MW00941469

CALVARY
CHURCH

WWW.CALVARY.US

TABLE OF CONTENTS

Acknowledgements   2

Introduction   3

Chapter One: *Let's Grow!*   5

Chapter Two: *Delight in God's Truth* (Bible Study)   23

Chapter Three: *Yield Some Time to God* (Praying)   41

Chapter Four: *Nurture Authentic Community*   61
         (Connecting with Others)

Chapter Five: *Actively Serve Others* (Serving)   77

Chapter Six: *Magnify God with Passion* (Worship)   95

Chapter Seven: *Invest in God's Kingdom* (Giving)   111

Chapter Eight: *Contagiously Influence Others*   131
         (Sharing Your Faith)

Conclusion   153

Resources   154

ACKNOWLEDGEMENTS

Like all worthwhile endeavors, this project was a team effort. I am extremely grateful for the talented team I have the privilege of serving with at Calvary. They have a great passion for helping people grow spiritually, and it was their insight and encouragement that convinced me to rewrite and update this book and lead our church on another *Discover Dynamic Life* campaign.

Pastor Danny Bennett and Donna Foster sifted through the material and video lessons to help produce the small group curriculum. Some of our ministry assistants provided administrative support, especially Janis Russell and Deborah Jensen. Jason Lazzaro, our Graphics Specialist, designed the graphic look of the entire campaign, the book covers, and laid out the materials for print.

Our worship team stepped up to help produce the video lessons. They spent some long evenings listening and encouraging. I am grateful to Chris Bennett, Francisco Vargas, Gary Apple, and, of course, Pastor Greg Toney. Dave Moser at Kelby Media in Oldsmar graciously offered us their studios for videoing, and several members of their team helped us immeasurably. We are grateful for their support of our work.

INTRODUCTION

The Christian life is about growth. Spiritual maturity is a process. You must grow into the meaningful life Jesus created for you. One of the tragedies in churches today is the vast number of believers who have not grown. Year after year their spiritual life remains dull and lethargic. They bear little or no fruit. No wonder they are bored and discontent. Deep within their hearts they sense there is more. Yet they are not sure where or how to find it. Sadly, many have been open, but often leaders and churches have failed to push them onward toward real spiritual depth. Sometimes they think the answer lies in a new mystical experience, or some new doctrine or clever teacher. But the answer, as always, lies with Jesus. This book and series is about getting to know Him better. It is about the life-long habits you need to grow spiritually and keep growing.

I want to invite you on an eight-week journey. It is a journey of discovery and realization. You do not have to stay where you are. You can discover the fullness of life Jesus offers. Isn't it time to step up to the next level? So let's take the journey, and working together, we can discover dynamic life.

Chapter One

Let's Grow

My purpose is to give life in all its fullness.
John 10:10 (NLT)

DISCOVERING DYNAMIC LIFE

You were made for God. You were made by Him and for Him. The Bible says, *...all things have been created through him and for him* (Colossians 1:16 NIV).

And that's it. That's where you find the secret to life, the meaning of life and the purpose of life. You were made by God to fulfill His purposes. Without God you're nothing more than an accidental life form, a highly evolved animal. Every thought about meaning, beauty and love is just some imaginary biological impulse. You came from nowhere, have no meaning, and you're headed nowhere. And no, that doesn't make sense. You know it doesn't.

You know better. You know there is more to life. The Bible says God has placed eternity in our hearts. Jesus said we can't live by bread (physical) alone, but by every word that proceeds from the mouth of God (spiritual). We think spiritual thoughts and wonder about the big questions of life. Where did you come from? Why are you here? Where are you going? The big questions can only be answered with God. And that does make sense.

The Bible says that you were made by God. You were created a spiritual being. You were made to know and serve Him. That's dynamic life. The word *dynamic* means living, powerful, meaningful, vibrant, healthy, and strong. That is the kind of life that God wants for you.

And that is what this book is all about. This is an invitation to *Discover Dynamic Life.* This is the life God made you for, the life you've always hungered for, and the life Jesus came to give. Jesus said, *I have come that they might have life and have it more abundantly.* (John 10:10) (NIV)

SPIRITUAL HEALTH

This book is about how to find that life and then grow in your relationship with God. Spiritual life is a lot like physical life. You didn't make yourself come alive. You didn't choose when and where you would be born. Your life comes from somewhere or someone else. The same thing is true with spiritual life. You can't produce it. It comes from God. Spiritual health is a lot like physical health. There are some things you can control, and some things you can't. Some things you can't change, but some things you can change. If you're going to be spiritually healthy, and if you're going to grow spiritually, you have to work on the things you can control. You trust God to do what only He can do, but you have to do your part to grow stronger.

This book is about both. It's about understanding the things that only God can do and trusting Him to work in your life according to His purpose and power. But it's especially about the things you can control. It's about learning how to grow so that you can discover all God has for you.

First, let's talk about what only God can do.

REAL LIFE COMES FROM GOD

The philosopher/theologian Blaise Pascal wrote about the search for happiness. He said,

> *What else does this craving, and this helplessness, proclaim but that there was once in man a true happiness, of which all that now remains is the empty print and trace? This he tries in vain to fill with everything around him, seeking in things that are not there the help he cannot find in those that are, though none can help, since this*

infinite abyss can be filled only with an infinite and immutable object; in other words by God himself.[1]

There is a hole, a vacuum in life, which only God can fill. You are created for God, and until you find Him and know Him, there will be emptiness in your heart that nothing else can fill. Proverbs 14:12 says, *There is a way that seems right to a man, but in the end it leads to death* (NIV).

We look for all kind of things to fill the need for meaning and purpose in our lives. We look for fulfillment, but we tend to look in the wrong places. The Bible says,

> *Do not love the world or the things in the world. If anyone loves the world, the love of the Father is not in him. For all that is in the world — the lust of the flesh, the lust of the eyes, and the pride of life — is not of the Father but is of the world. And the world is passing away, and the lust of it; but he who does the will of God abides forever.* 1 John 2:15-17 NKJV

People have not changed. We have the same needs and the same tendencies. In fact according to the Bible, people have always searched for happiness and fulfillment in other things; specifically, in three areas.

PLEASURE

The first is *the lust of the flesh*. The New Living Translation (NLT) says *the lust for physical pleasure*. The first substitute for God is *pleasure*. There is nothing wrong with pleasure. God created us to experience pleasure and wants us to know pleasure.

---

[1] Pascal, Blaise. *Pensées*. (New York: Penguin Books, 1966).

But feeling good for a moment has never made anyone truly happy. When our desire for pleasure gets out of control and out of balance it ends up doing more harm than good. The devil wants to corrupt what God intended for good and use it to bring destruction in our lives. This is what happens when people get addicted to alcohol or drugs, or even sexual behaviors. Gradually a momentary pleasure begins to produce a lifetime of pain. When pleasure becomes our god, it is sure to lead us to a lifetime of bondage. Even when we avoid the pitfalls of addictive behaviors, pleasure alone is not enough for real happiness. Plenty of people have spent their lives chasing the "good feeling" only to look back at a wasted life devoid of real purpose. Pleasure is no substitute for God.

POSSESSIONS

The second alternative for God is described as *the lust of the eyes*. The NLT says *the lust for everything we see*. The second false substitute for God is *possessions*. We want more. We fall into the trap of believing that life is about accumulating more stuff: more toys, more money, more things. Many of us live believing that if we just had a little more we would be happy. Someone once asked a very wealthy man, *How much is enough?* His response was, *just a little more*.

Money isn't evil. It can be used for good or bad. There are rich people who love God and poor people who ignore God and vice versa. But the Bible does say, *For the love of money is the root of all evil* (1 Timothy 6:10 KJV).

It is greed that causes us to want more and more and be dissatisfied with what we do have. Materialism corrupts our perspective, robs us of gratitude, and deceives us into believing that if we only had more, maybe we could finally be fulfilled. But if you think about it, you know it isn't true. We've all gotten that new "thing" (car, outfit, house, toy) only to discover that after a short while the "new" wears off and we're longing for something else to make us feel excited again.

When I was in college, a bunch of guys went out one night to a dog track in Greene County, Alabama. For the first and only time in my life I watched dogs racing around the track while people sat in the stands betting on which dog would win. I noticed that the dogs chased a mechanical rabbit, and I asked one of the workers what would happen if a dog ever caught the rabbit. He said it would be a very bad thing, and that when it occasionally happened the dog that caught the mechanical rabbit was through racing. I asked why. He said because the dog then realized that the rabbit was fake; it wasn't worth having. So I watched the dogs chasing a fake rabbit around a track, a rabbit that they weren't likely to catch, and one that if it were ever caught it would only disappoint. Then I looked at the people in the stands. I looked at the dogs, and then the people. Dogs … people. It occurred to me that the people gambling weren't much different than the dogs on the track. They were all chasing something they couldn't catch, and if by some chance they did catch what they were chasing, they would find out it wasn't worth having after all. You'll never have enough money to satisfy your deepest cravings. Money is no substitute for God.

PRIDE

The third substitute for God is *pride*. I John 2:16 calls it the *pride of life.* You look for fulfillment in importance or success. You think that if only you could be somebody famous and important, or if only you could have that title, or if only you could accomplish that elusive goal, then finally you would be fulfilled. We crave the applause and admiration of others and believe that if we could have them, we would finally be happy. I think part of this is what is behind the popularity of reality shows. People parade their lives in front of others because they want to be known; they want to be famous. But if fame and popularity are all we think they are, then why are so many famous people so messed up? Why do so many of their relationships fail? Why are there so many psychologists in Hollywood? Because fame is no guarantee of happiness. In fact, it usually brings a new share of problems.

This is also why so many people chase after success. It isn't just money. We often think, "If I could just be somebody important in the eyes of others, it would verify my importance and meaning." We spend our lives trying to impress people we don't even know or like; only to find out they aren't that impressed anyway. Often people spend their lives trying to impress people they don't like and end up losing the respect of the ones who really did love them just for who they were. Feeling important and accomplished is no substitute for God.

REAL FULFILLMENT

These same three temptations have always been around. It is what Satan tempted Adam and Eve with. Think about it. She *saw* the forbidden fruit (lust of the eyes) and that it was *good for food* (lust of the flesh), and they wanted to *become like God* (pride of life). These were the same three temptations Satan used on Jesus with decidedly different results. He tempted Him with the kingdoms of the world (lust of the eyes), with turning the stones into bread (lust of the flesh), and with jumping off of the temple so that angels would swoop down and catch Him (pride of life). Adam and Eve said yes to all three, and so have all of us. But Jesus said no to all three, which is why we need His help.

Here's the problem with looking for fulfillment in those three areas. They are no substitute for God. Yes, they can produce happiness, but it doesn't last. Look at what John said, *And the world is passing away* (1 John 2:17). The problem with all of these substitutes for fulfillment is that whatever fulfillment they provide is fleeting. It is like eating a sumptuous meal or quenching a raging thirst. You feel satisfied for a little while, but it doesn't take long and you are hungry or thirsty again.

Now compare that with what Jesus showed a Samaritan woman about finding real fulfillment.

> *When a Samaritan woman came to draw water, Jesus said to her, "Will you give me a drink?" (His disciples had gone into the town to buy food.) The Samaritan woman said to him, "You are a Jew and I am a Samaritan woman. How can you ask me for a drink?" (For Jews do not associate with Samaritans.) Jesus answered her, "If you knew the gift of God and who it is that asks you for a drink, you would have asked him and he would have given you living water." "Sir," the woman said, "you have nothing to draw with and the well is deep. Where can you get this living water? Are you greater than our father Jacob, who gave us the well and drank from it himself, as did also his sons and his flocks and herds?" Jesus answered, "Everyone who drinks this water will be thirsty again, but whoever drinks the water I give him will never thirst. Indeed, the water I give him will become in him a spring of water welling up to eternal life." The woman said to him, "Sir, give me this water so that I won't get thirsty and have to keep coming here to draw water." John 4:7-15 NIV*

The Samaritan woman came looking for water; she wanted to quench a physical thirst — nothing wrong with that. You have physical appetites that need to be quenched. God gave you those appetites for your good, and even your pleasure. But quenching your thirst isn't enough for inner fulfillment. Jesus pointed out the inadequacy of physical pleasure by observing that whoever drank the water from the well would become thirsty again. Physical pleasures only satisfy for a short time, and then you are hungry all over again.

Can you remember some of the Thanksgiving meals you've enjoyed? Remember sitting down to a sumptuous feast of turkey, mashed potatoes, dressing, and gravy… getting hungry yet? And then, of course, five different pies for dessert! Forget restraint; you just plow in and enjoy everything you can. Finally you push yourself away from the table and roll into an overstuffed chair for some football and a nap. Then you inevitably say something like, "I can't eat another bite!" You might even say, "I won't eat again for days." But you know better. A couple of hours later, you are back for another piece of pie and a turkey sandwich. Even if you make it through the day, tomorrow comes and you're hungry all over again, just like you never ate to begin with. Physical appetites only stay quenched for a little while, and then we're hungry or thirsty all over again.

That is why Jesus said, *Everyone who drinks this water will be thirsty again*. But then Jesus offered something different. He said, *But whoever drinks the water I give him will never thirst. Indeed, the water I give him will become in him a spring of water welling up to eternal life*. Jesus was clearly speaking about more than physical realities. When He spoke of a spring of water welling up to eternal life, He made it clear He was speaking of something spiritual; something that would quench our inner thirst forever. He is the ultimate solution to our spiritual hunger. He is the one our soul craves.

We look for life in all kinds of things and in all kind of places, but God offers us real life and lasting fulfillment.

Consider the following verses:

- *But He answered and said, "It is written, 'Man shall not live by bread alone, but by every word that proceeds from the mouth of God.'"* Matthew 4:4, NKJV

- *He who has the Son has life; he who does not have the Son of God does not have life.* 1 John 5:12, NIV

Real life comes from God. You didn't create your physical life, and you can't create spiritual life either. It comes from God. Only He can make you spiritually alive. But here's the good news: God does offer that life. He offers it freely. He offers it to anyone. He offers it to you. He offers it through Jesus.

NEW LIFE

The reason there is a natural separation between you and God is because of what the Bible calls sin. We have all sinned. God came in Jesus to rescue us. His death on the cross paid the price for our sin, and the Bible says that God now offers us forgiveness and new life in Jesus. Spiritual life begins in us when we recognize our sin and our need for God. When we respond to Jesus in faith, turn away from our sin and give Him control of our life, the Bible says that a new life begins in us. The Bible says, *Therefore, if anyone is in Christ, he is a new creation. The old has passed away; behold, the new has come* (2 Corinthians 5:17 ESV).

In this book, we're going to talk about how you can grow in your spiritual life, how you can have dynamic life, but it has to start with a work of God in your life. If you have never trusted Him to save you, to forgive you, to give you new life, do it now. Let God make you come alive spiritually through faith in Jesus.

Your new life in Christ begins when you recognize your sin and guilt before God. You realize you need God's help and forgiveness and believe that Jesus is the Lord, God's one and only Son, who came to rescue you. He died for your sin and rose from the dead. When you believe this in your heart and then ask God to forgive you and take control of your life, you are saved from sin and given new life in Jesus. If you need to place your faith in Jesus, I hope you will do it now. Once you do trust Christ, you begin a new relationship with God. You need to grow in that relationship, and that is a continual process.

REAL LIFE REQUIRES CONTINUAL GROWTH

Jesus gives you real life. But here's a question, do you get it all at once or little by little? How about both? When Jesus comes to live within you and gives you real life, you are completely forgiven, completely brought into God's family, and secure in your relationship with Jesus. It's done. That is why we can speak of salvation in the past tense; we have been saved.

But is that all? No. Obviously when a person first comes to Christ, they don't know everything there is to know about following Christ or obeying Him. Some things we learn little by little. If spiritual growth were automatic, then every Christian would grow spiritually, and every Christian would grow into spiritual maturity at the same rate.

Spiritual growth is not automatic. In fact, some Christians fail to grow as quickly as they should, and they stay spiritually immature. In Hebrews 5, the Bible says,

There is so much more we would like to say about this. But you don't seem to listen, so it's hard to make you understand. You have been Christians a long time now, and you ought to be teaching others. Instead, you need

15

someone to teach you again the basic things a beginner must learn about the Scriptures. You are like babies who drink only milk and cannot eat solid food. And a person who is living on milk isn't very far along in the Christian life and doesn't know much about doing what is right. Solid food is for those who are mature, who have trained themselves to recognize the difference between right and wrong and do what is right. Hebrews 5:11-14 NLT

There are two truths in this passage about spiritual growth. First, spiritual growth is not automatic. In Hebrews 5, the readers were being rebuked because they should have grown faster and gone farther than they had. So we know it isn't automatic.

Second, spiritual growth is a process. It doesn't happen all at once. This passage talks about those who are spiritually immature and those who are mature. Just as it takes time to grow from an infant into an adult, it takes time to grow spiritually. It doesn't happen all at once. Notice how the Bible also speaks of those who had *trained themselves.* That means spiritual growth requires training and effort.

Now let's look at another passage. Look at what the Bible says in Philippians 2,

> *…work out your own salvation with fear and trembling; for it is God who works in you both to will and to do for His good pleasure.* Philippians 2:12-13 NKJV

Notice that there are two forces working to create spiritual growth. In verse 12, you are instructed to *work out your own salvation.* Who does the work? You do. Now that doesn't mean you earn forgiveness, or have to earn God's favor. You can't do that. You can only receive forgiveness. But once you have, there is work you must do if you are to grow spiritually.

In verse 13 it says it is *God who works in you.* Who is

doing the work? God is. God is at work in you to accomplish His will and purpose for your life. One way of looking at it is this: You can only *work out* what God has *worked in*. You can't produce spiritual growth on your own; God has to work in you first. But spiritual growth is not going to happen if you don't work in cooperation with God's purposes.

Salvation is a theological word that describes what God does for you when He forgives you and makes you a part of His family for eternity. Sanctification is a theological term that describes the process that takes place over time when you become more and more like Jesus. Salvation happens in a moment. Sanctification happens over time. Salvation is God's work. Sanctification is God's work, but it also involves you working. Your obedience makes a difference. There are things you can do and must do to grow spiritually, and there are things that, if neglected, will affect your spiritual health. If you want to grow you have to work with God who is already working in you to make it happen.

SPIRITUAL GROWTH REQUIRES WORK

"Let's work out." You know what that means. It's time to go to the gym or the track and do some physical exercise. Most people know that if they are going to get physically strong or remain physically strong, they need to exercise. There are things you can do to make a difference in your physical health. The same thing is true spiritually. You need to work out. This isn't a one-time thing anymore than you can exercise once and forget about it. It is a lifestyle choice, or maybe for you a lifestyle change. You need a spiritual workout.

Now imagine heading into the gym. Imagine you're a novice with the weight machines and exercise regimens. A trainer comes along and begins to write a workout program for you; a series of exercises and goals that will help you develop physical health. Sometimes you just need a little help, a little instruction. That is the purpose of this book. We're going to work out. More than that, I want to help you know how to keep working out so that you can grow stronger and stronger with God.

Working out takes discipline. Let's face it, everyone would like to have a perfectly toned body and be in top physical shape, but most of us struggle with discipline. It takes discipline to exercise, eat right, and stay in shape. It also takes discipline to stay and grow spiritually healthy. Notice the connection between the word *disciple* and the word *discipline*. Jesus calls us to a life of discipleship. *And anyone who does not carry his cross and follow me cannot be my disciple* (Luke 14:27 NIV).

SEVEN DISCIPLINES

Discipline, disciple, and discipleship all come from the same root word. To be a disciple of Christ requires discipline. To be specific, it requires seven disciplines. You find them in God's Word. While these seven disciplines are found throughout the Bible, you can see them all in a snapshot of the early church in Acts 2. These early followers of Jesus engaged in seven disciplines that helped them grow spiritually strong, and their growth fueled a movement which rocked the world. You need to learn these seven disciplines and apply them to your life. If you do, you will grow stronger.

So come alongside these spiritual champions and let's watch them working out their faith.

Peter replied, "Repent and be baptized, every one of you, in the name of Jesus Christ for the forgiveness of your sins. And you will receive the gift of the Holy Spirit. The promise is for you and your children and for all who are far off — for all whom the Lord our God will call." With many other words he warned them; and he pleaded with them, "Save yourselves from this corrupt generation." Those who accepted his message were baptized, and about three thousand were added to their number that day. They devoted themselves to the apostles' teaching and to the fellowship, to the breaking of bread and to prayer. Everyone was filled with awe, and many wonders and miraculous signs were done by the apostles. All the believers were together and had everything in common. Selling their possessions and goods, they gave to anyone as he had need. Every day they continued to meet together in the temple courts. They broke bread in their homes and ate together with glad and sincere hearts, praising God and enjoying the favor of all the people. And the Lord added to their number daily those who were being saved. [emphases added] Acts 2:38-47 NIV

Let's see if we can unlock their secret to spiritual health. Look at the things they did, the verbs, and discover their workout routine. Notice seven key disciplines.

Maybe the first thing you notice is that they *devoted themselves to the apostles' teaching.* The apostles were teaching the Scriptures, the Bible. They taught from the Hebrew Scriptures, which we know today as the Old Testament. They were also studying the life of Jesus and writing down what it meant to live as followers of Christ, which is what became our New Testament. They were learning spiritual truth from what we know today as the Bible. The first discipline is Bible Study.

Next, notice the emphasis on prayer. These early believers learned to talk to God by meeting with each other and praying. They listened while others prayed and learned to pray themselves. So the second discipline is prayer.

Then notice the emphasis on *fellowship... the breaking of bread,* and then the phrase in verse 46: *They broke bread in their homes and ate together.* Okay, so they ate together. What does that mean? It means they were building close, personal, authentic relationships with each other. So the third discipline for spiritual growth is building authentic friendships with other believers.

The next discipline is found in the phrase *they gave.* Generous giving flowed out of their lives as they expressed their love for each other and their love for God. Since we all struggle with greed and materialism, we all need this discipline. The fourth discipline is generous giving.

The fifth discipline is found in the phrase *to anyone as he had need.* Their giving flowed to meet the needs that people had. They were sensitive to each other's needs, and in their community they met each other's needs. That's what ministry is, serving each other and meeting needs in the name of Jesus. That's the fifth discipline, serving.

The next discipline is found in the phrase *praising God.* Verse 46 also says they met together for worship in the temple courts. Public, corporate worship was an important part of their lives, and it continued to be indispensable to their spiritual health. So the sixth discipline is worship.

Finally, look at how they had an impact on those outside their community of faith, unbelievers. The Bible says in verse 40 that Peter *warned them; and he pleaded with them.* Peter communicated the message of faith to unbelievers and showed them how to repent of their sins and put their faith in Jesus. He communicated his faith to others and had a contagious influence. Verses 46-47 adds, *and enjoying the favor of all the people. And the Lord added to their number daily those who were being saved.* God worked through the witness of these early believers to continually draw more and more people into the faith. The church exploded with influence and growth. The last discipline is sharing your faith with others.

There are the seven disciplines that produce dynamic spiritual life. These are the seven disciplines that need to become part of your regular workout routine to help you work out your salvation. Wherever you are on your spiritual journey, I want to help you understand these seven disciplines, apply them to your life, and grow in dynamic life.

In order to help you remember and study these habits we developed an acrostic based on these seven disciplines to help you discover D-Y-N-A-M-I-C life. Dynamic life is characterized by these seven disciplines:

D- Delights in God's Truth (Bible Study)
Y- Yields Some Time to God (Praying)
N- Nurtures Authentic Community (Connecting with Others)
A- Actively Serves Others (Serving)
M- Magnifies God with Passion (Worship)
I- Invests in God's Kingdom (Giving)
C- Contagiously Influences Others (Sharing Faith)

Remember what Jesus promised? He promised life in all "fullness," life to the max. This is the dynamic life Jesus promised, but it only comes when you are willing to do your part, the workout. Jesus paid the price for it and offers it free, but now you must seize it. Over the next several chapters you are going to learn how to grow and develop your own personal workout plan for spiritual growth.

One of the best things you can do to make the most of *Discover Dynamic Life* is to do it as part of a small group and/or a church-wide emphasis where you are learning alongside others. You can also work through this material with another believer one-on-one who is investing their time in you and helping you grow spiritually. If you are not part of a group or aren't working with another believer one-on-one, you can still learn and grow as you study each of these seven disciplines. But, as you will see, one of those disciplines is connecting with other believers in a meaningful way.

I hope you will take time after each chapter to pause and really think about that discipline in your life. There is always room to grow, and even if you've been a Christian a long time, there are always new steps in each area that you can take to continue to grow in Christ. If you are a new Christian, or if you have recently made a fresh commitment to grow spiritually, then this is a perfect time to discover the disciplines of dynamic life. Ready, set, let's grow!

Chapter Two

Delight in God's Truth
The Discipline of Bible Study

I have hidden your word in my heart that I
might not sin against you.
Psalm 119:11 (NIV)

REVELATION

In 1999, John F. Kennedy, Jr., the famous, handsome, successful son of the former President, became another Kennedy family tragedy. This time it was not an assassin's bullet, but a fatal error that caused the tragedy. Kennedy was killed when the private plane he was piloting crashed over the Atlantic Ocean as he was headed to Martha's Vineyard for a family wedding celebration.

On July 16th, he, his wife Carolyn, and her sister Lauren boarded the Piper Saratoga and began what should have been a short uneventful flight from the Essex County airport in New Jersey to the island off the Massachusetts coast. The weather seemed clear, and even though Kennedy was not certified to fly at night, there seemed to be no doubt he could, or would, arrive on the resort island in time. No one knows exactly what occurred, but the National Transportation Safety Board later concluded that pilot error was the probable cause.[2]

Every pilot knows about spatial disorientation, which can lead to what is commonly called "the death spiral." When a pilot flies the plane, it is very easy to become disoriented. It is possible to not even know up from down, right from left or even if you are spinning or flying level. Every pilot knows that ultimately you don't trust your senses; you trust the instrument panel. A pilot who flies according to his senses, according to what feels right or seems right, will almost certainly face inevitable tragedy.

It is easy to become disoriented in flying and also in life. There are two ways to know the truth about life, speculation or revelation. Speculation is when you or

---

[2] "John F. Kennedy, Jr. plane crash," Wikipedia. http://en.wikipedia.org/wiki/John_F._Kennedy,_Jr._plane_crash (accessed 16 Dec. 2011).

someone else makes a guess. Revelation is when someone wiser than you, someone like God, reveals truth. The Bible is God's truth to us. It is unlike any other book, even other religious books. The Bible wasn't compiled by just one man (such as the Koran or the Book of Mormon) but by more than 40 men over 1,500 years, and yet the Bible has one theme. It is God's plan for humankind. We see God at work through His people, Israel, and then God coming in Jesus to fulfill His plan. We see God forming His church, instructing His people, and picturing a victorious future and glorious eternity. Every type of human condition is pictured. The questions we wrestle with are apparent; it is the story of saints and sinners, losers and winners, doubt and faith, obedience and disobedience. Yet through it all God points the way to an intimate relationship with Him and the path to victorious life. If you want the dynamic life that God created for you, you must learn to *delight in God's truth*.

This is the first discipline of dynamic life and in some ways it is the most important. Every other discipline flows from this one. Every other discipline is taught in the Bible. If you start and succeed here, then eventually you will get all the rest.

Most Christians know they need to read the Bible, but many just don't know how. Maybe you're like that. Perhaps you've tried but it didn't make sense. Maybe you got started but got stuck in Leviticus. Maybe it seemed boring. (It's OK to admit it; God knows anyway.) Relax, you can do this, and your spiritual growth depends on it. Wherever you're starting from, we'll help. The Bible isn't just for pastors and religious experts; it is God's word for YOU. You can read it. You can understand it. You can learn to delight in God's truth.

Why do I use the word *delight*? Because the Bible does. You need to do more than just read it and be exposed to it; you must learn to delight in it.

Psalm 119 is the longest chapter in the Bible — 176 verses. Yet, it has one theme; God's Word. In fact, the chapter is written like an acrostic. If you look in your Bible you will see 22 sections in the chapter, and each is headed with a Hebrew word. Actually, it is a Hebrew letter, and those 22 letters form the Hebrew alphabet. In each section, the first word starts with that particular letter. Imagine writing a children's A-B-C book where you have a paragraph for each section that begins with that letter. Well, that's what Psalm 119 is, but the theme of each of the 22 sections is how wonderful God's Word is. Check out these verses from Psalm 119.

- *I will delight in your principles and not forget your word.* Psalm 119:16 NLT

- *Your testimonies also are my delight and my counselors.* Psalm 119:24 NKJV

- *Direct me in the path of your commands, for there I find delight.* Psalm 119:35 NIV

- *And I will delight myself in your commandments, which I love.* Psalm 119:47 NKJV

- *But I delight in your law.* Psalm 119:70 NLT

- *Let your compassion come to me that I may live, for your law is my delight.* Psalm 119:77 NIV

- *If your law had not been my delight, I would have perished in my affliction.* Psalm 119:92 NIV

- *Oh, how I love your law! I think about it all day long.* Psalm 119:97 NLT

- *I long for your salvation, O LORD, and your law is my delight.* Psalm 119:174 NKJV

Now circle the word "delight" (or its closest synonym) in each verse. Do you see how important it is to delight in God's truth? Now if you look closely at Psalm 119 there are three things involved in delighting in God's truth.

ACCEPT GOD'S WORD AS TRUTH

What do you look to for guidance? Where is your objective standard for right and wrong? How do you separate truth from deception? Where is your control panel? The Bible is a control panel you can trust. It is a foundation on which you can build your life. It is a guide you can follow. The Bible says, *Thy word is a lamp unto my feet and a light unto my path* (Psalm 119:105 NKJV).

The Bible is true. It is inspired by God. Look at what the Bible says,

> *All Scripture is given by inspiration of God, and is profitable for doctrine, for reproof, for correction, for instruction in righteousness,* 2 Timothy 3:16 NKJV

Now circle the word *inspiration.* It is the Greek word *Theópneustos.* Now look at the first part of the word. *Theo* comes from *Theos,* which means God. Now look at the second part of the word. The word *pneustos* comes from *pneo,* which means to breathe. A related word *pneuma* not only means breathe, but can also be used of the Holy Spirit. So literally the word *inspired* means God-breathed. According to the Bible, God literally breathed His words, His truth, into the lives of His servants who wrote according to His direct will. According to 2 Peter, *It was the Holy*

Spirit who moved the prophets to speak from God (2 Peter 1:21 NLT).

How do you know God's Word is true? First, it is believed by faith. As in all spiritual things, *without faith it is impossible to please God, because anyone who comes to him must believe that he exists and that he rewards those who earnestly seek him.* (Hebrews 11:6 NIV).

The Bible tells us that the Israelites missed out on the Promised Land, initially, because they refused to accept God's Word (Psalm 106:24). Their lack of faith caused them to miss out on God's promises. While some people will scoff at the necessity of faith, the truth is that most of what we believe we accept on some level by faith. You have to choose whom you will trust. You can trust yourself, you can trust someone else, or you can trust God. You can make your choice, but you still trust someone. Even if you say, "I'll only believe it if I can see it or prove it," you are still trusting your own wisdom, senses, and discernment. Remember the pilot? Trust your own senses if you want to, but you can still be deceived and the consequences can be catastrophic.

While we accept God's Word by faith, it is also important to know that it is a reasonable faith. God gave us a mind and invites us to know wisdom. He says, *Get wisdom! Understand! Do not forget, nor turn away from the words of my mouth* (Proverbs 4:5 NKJV).

SCRIPTURAL EVIDENCE

It is a reasonable thing to believe that God's Word is true. There have been many scoffers and skeptics who have tried to disprove God's Word and declared it was out of date, or perhaps that some scientific discovery had relegated it as irrelevant. Yet, those loud voices seem to come and go, and God's Word still stands true. Again and again scientific or historic discoveries only confirm the facts in the Bible and strengthen the faith of a whole new generation.

You should believe the Bible is true because of the scriptural evidence. The Bible claims to be true. (Psalm 119:160)

Jesus placed great weight upon the Scriptures and believed them to be the very words of God. Jesus said,

> *Don't misunderstand why I have come. I did not come to abolish the law of Moses or the writings of the prophets. No, I came to accomplish their purpose. I tell you the truth, until heaven and earth disappear, not even the smallest detail of God's law will disappear until its purpose is achieved.*
> Matthew 5:17-18 NLT

HISTORICAL RELIABILITY

The cynic could correctly observe that believing the Bible is true just because it claims to be true is not proof. That kind of logic is sometimes called circular reasoning. Fair enough. But it is important to establish that we are not claiming more for the Bible than the Bible claims for itself. The Bible does claim to be true, the words of God, and if you are predisposed to trust the Bible, then that is a good place to at least begin.

But there are many reasons to believe the Bible is true. The Bible is a book about historical people and historical places. The history described extensively in the Bible has been confirmed again and again by archeology. Unlike some books that are merely myth and legend, the Bible references many historical events that can and have been verified by independent archeological evidence.

Recently, a 2,500 year-old tablet was translated that contained the name of a little-known Babylonian official

who lived over 500 years before Christ[3]. What was signify-
cant is that the name corresponds to a verse in the Bible,
Jeremiah 39:3, which says,

> *Then all the officials of the king of Babylon came and took*
> *seats in the Middle gate: Nergal-Sharezer of Samgar,*
> *Nebo-Sarsekim a chief officer, Nergal-Sharezer a high*
> *official and all the other officials of the king of Babylon.*

Now, that verse may not seem that exciting, except
that officials at the British Museum recently announced that
the 2,500-year-old cuneiform dating to 595 B.C. contained
the name of Nebo-Sarsekim and his title as chief eunuch of
the Babylonian king. A British Museum official named
Irving Finkel was quoted in the London Telegraph as saying,
This is a fantastic discovery, a world class find. If Nebo-Sarsekim
existed, which other lesser figures in the Old Testament existed? A
throwaway detail in the Old Testa- ment turns out to be accurate
and true. I think it means that the whole of the narrative (of
Jeremiah) takes on a new kind of power.[4]

Now, you may not need a Babylonian tablet to
confirm your faith in the Bible's accuracy, but isn't it neat
that again and again science and archeology seem to be
catching up to what the Bible has said all along? God's Word
is true, down to the smallest detail.

The Bible is the most well documented book in anti-
quity. There are over 5,000 ancient Greek manuscripts of the
biblical text, and there is no other ancient book that even
comes close. The Bible, unlike other religious writings, is not
the product of one man. The Bible was composed over 1,500
years by 40 different authors on 3 different continents in 3

---

[3] "Nebo-Sarsekim Found in Babylonian Tablet." *Bible and Spade Magazine.*
Summer 2007.

[4] Willis, Avery. *Masterlife.* (Nashville: Broadman & Holman, 1988).

different languages. It is the bestselling book of all time.

There are amazing prophecies in the Bible that have been fulfilled. There are over 60 prophecies in the Old Testament that were fulfilled in the life of Jesus.

PERSONAL TESTIMONIES

Maybe the greatest evidence for the Bible is the practical evidence. The proof is in the pudding. The Bible has impacted more lives for good than any other book in all of history. Judge for yourself. Why is it that the most grounded, fulfilled, and happy people are often the very ones who love the Bible and take its message seriously? Do you know anyone who really messed their life up because they read the Bible and tried to apply it to their life? The Bible is true and it can be trusted.

There is much more that can be studied and investigated regarding the truthfulness of the Bible. It is beyond the scope of this discussion. If you are looking for some rational evidence to strengthen your faith in the Bible, check out Lee Strobel's book *The Case for Faith*[5]. Several of the chapters deal with the truthfulness of the Bible and how the search for truth led the author, a former hardened agnostic, to accept the truth about the Bible and the truth about Jesus. Another classic is Josh McDowell's book *Evidence that Demands a Verdict*[6].

If you are struggling with accepting the Bible as truth, talk to a Bible Study leader, a spiritual mentor or pastor and ask them for more resources to research. Most of all, just read the Bible for yourself. Many skeptics who

---

[5] Strobel, Lee. *The Case for Faith.* (Grand Rapids: Zondervan, 2000).

[6] McDowell, Josh. Evidence that Demands a Verdict. (Nashville: Thomas Nelson, 1999).

started out doubting the Bible have been converted just because they decided to read it for themselves. Don't take someone else's word; check it out. Read it for yourself, and I am convinced you will see for yourself that the Bible is a reliable guide that can be trusted.

Once you accept the truthfulness of the Bible, then move on to the second key in delighting in God's truth: reading and studying it for yourself.

PUT GOD'S WORD INTO YOUR HEART

The Bible is truth, but it only makes a difference if you get it into your life. Look at Psalm 119:11 again.

What is the result of getting God's Word into your heart? It is victory over sin, or to put it another way, dynamic life. In the story of Jesus' temptation in Matthew 4:1-11, Jesus responded to every temptation by quoting the Bible.

So, how do you get God's Word operating in your life, your heart? Avery Willis was a missionary who authored the *Master Life* discipleship course several years ago. He used the acrostic H-E-A-R-T to illustrate the five ways to get God's Word deeply into your heart.

H- Hearing God's Word

So then faith comes by hearing, and hearing by the word of God. Romans 10:17 NKJV

Your first step is usually hearing God's Word. You hear it preached, taught, or discussed. You go to church and the pastor talks about the Bible and you hear God's truth, or you attend a Bible study where someone teaches and leads a discussion. They are talking and you are hearing. Hearing is almost always the first step in coming to faith in Christ. Hearing is an important first step, but it is only the first step.

You can improve your hearing by being faithful to attend worship, by getting involved in a Life Group or Bible Study where the Bible is taught, by listening to sermons on the radio or television, by downloading audio files and even taking notes when you are listening.

While listening is a great first step, it is sad that many Christians never get beyond that basic step. All they know about God's Word is what they've heard or what they've been told. While you can come to faith that way, it is hard to grow spiritually mature that way. If all you ever do is listen to what someone else says about God's Word, you will probably stay spiritually immature and even prone to deception and false teaching. You need to go to the next step.

E- Examining God's Word

And it shall be with him, and he shall read it all the days of his life, that he may learn to fear the LORD his God and be careful to observe all the words of this law and these statutes.
Deuteronomy 17:19 NKJV

Examining God's Word means you read it for yourself. You need to learn to read the Bible on your own. Maybe the Bible seems confusing and hard to read. Sometimes it is, but there are some simple steps you can take to learn to read the Bible on your own.

Read it systematically. Don't just open the Bible and start reading wherever. You need to understand the context of every passage in order for it to make sense. So learn a system. Read through a particular book or passage. If you are just starting out, it probably isn't the best idea to start in Genesis and read all the way through, although you can and should work up to that.

If you are just starting out, I would recommend reading through books in the Bible in this order: John, 1 John, Galatians, Ephesians, Philippians, and Colossians. Then read though Proverbs. If you read one chapter of Proverbs a day, you can read through it in one month. Follow that with the book of Psalms. If you read 5 chapters of Psalms a day, you will read through it in one month. Then go back to the New Testament and read Luke, 1 and 2 Thessalonians, and 1 and 2 Timothy. By now you're ready to tackle Genesis. That is 14 books of the Bible, and that can easily take you a year or more.

Read a little each day and try to understand what you are reading before you move on. I also read through the Bible once each year. I've been doing that for many years. It isn't that hard to do if you're willing to read about five chapters a day. Here is how I do it. I read Genesis through Deuteronomy in the months of January and February. In March and April, I switch to the New Testament and read Matthew through Acts. I read from Joshua to Esther in the months of May and June. I read from Job to Song of Songs during July and August. I read from Romans to Colossians in September. In October and November, I read Isaiah to Malachi, and in December I finish with 1 Thessalonians to Revelation. I read that way so I can switch back and forth between the Old and New Testament throughout the year. The months help me stay on track so that if I get behind I know I need to catch up. If you read about five chapters a day, between 15-20 minutes, you will read through the entire Bible in a year.

Get a newer translation. Since the Bible was written primarily in Greek (New Testament) and Hebrew (Old Testament) it has to be translated into English. Some translations are older and harder to understand, while others are more current and easier to read. I recommend the New International Version (NIV) or the New Living Translation (NLT) for reading or reading aloud to others. The English Standard Version (ESV), New American Standard (NAS), and the New King James (NKJV) are great translations for serious study.

Purchase a study Bible. A study Bible contains notes and helpful tools to aid you in getting the most out of your Bible reading. Most translations come in a Study Bible format, and you can easily find good ones online or at a bookstore. If you have a friend, Bible study leader, or pastor, ask them for a recommendation.

If you are just getting started, consider using a devotional to keep you on track and guide you every day. A devotional can contain Bible readings for everyday and possibly contain some thoughts or comments for you to think about.

Now, to help you get started, as part of *Discover Dynamic Life* I've included a recommended list of Bible readings to help you over the next seven weeks. There are six passages a week to read, so if you miss a day you can still keep up, or if you want to look at a passage more closely you can do that. The passages I've given you go along with what you're learning in each chapter of this book. It's a great way to begin the habit of reading the Bible.

After you finish this book, consider reading through books of the Bible.

A – Analyzing God's Word

They received the message with great eagerness and examined the Scriptures every day to see if what Paul said was true.
Acts 17:11 NIV

Analyzing God's Word means to study it. The difference between reading and studying is that when you study you ask questions and write things down. Most people who study God's Word keep a notebook of some kind and the write down their questions and thoughts. Ask who, what, when, why, and where questions.

Of all the questions you ask, make sure you ask the "so what" question. This is when you want to find out, "What is this passage saying to me? What difference does this make in my life?"

As you grow more comfortable in studying the Bible you might consider using some tools that help you understand God's Word better. Some common tools people use include concordance, Bible dictionary, commentaries, and computer programs or applications.

A concordance lists Bible topics alphabetically and then gives you verses where those topics are found. For instance, you can look up the word faith and then find verses that have the word faith. Most study Bibles have a concordance in the back. An exhaustive concordance is one that contains every reference to a given word, whereas many concordances give a more limited selection of verses.

A Bible Dictionary is just like a normal dictionary except it focuses on Bible words, and it usually gives you more information than a normal dictionary. It's like a cross between a dictionary and an encyclopedia. When you look up a word in the Bible, you will find an article explaining what it means.

Commentaries are books written by someone about a book in the Bible. For instance if you have a commentary on the book of Matthew, it will go through the book of Matthew in order and provide that author's comments about each passage. Some commentaries are very academic in their orientation, while others are written in a way for a broader audience to understand. Commentaries are a great way to get other people's insights about difficult passages and topics. Most Study Bibles also include some commentary notes around each passage. Just remember that there is a difference between reading the Bible and reading what someone thinks about the Bible. A commentary is just another person's opinions or insights. It can be helpful, just keep it in perspective.

Today there are many computer programs and apps for Bible Study. Often these include the above tools as well as other helpful things like Hebrew and Greek Lexicons (explanations of Hebrew and Greek words), Interlinear Bibles (Bibles with the English passage and the original language together), maps, and illustrations. A computer program can be a significant investment, but it can also become a lifelong tool for enriched Bible learning. Talk to a Bible Study leader or pastor about what they use to get some good ideas.

R- Remembering God's Word

Keep my commands and live, and my law as the apple of your eye. Bind them on your fingers; Write them on the tablet of your heart. Proverbs 7:2-3 NKJV

Now, if you really want to go deep with God's Word, begin to memorize part of it. This is what it really means to get it into your heart. Now, most people think, "I can't memorize anything." Sure you can, you do it all the time. You memorize phone numbers, addresses, the lines from favorite songs, sports statistics, dates, and even your Social Security number. You know what you memorize? You memorize what is important to you!

God's Word helps you resist temptation, it helps you make wise decisions, strengthens you when you are under stress, encourages you when you are sad, and helps you share with other people. If God's Word can do all of that for you, doesn't it make sense that you would take a little time and effort to commit a few verses to memory? To help you begin memorizing scripture, I've also included a verse at the end of each chapter for you to memorize.

T- Thinking About God's Word

Blessed is the man ... his delight is in the law of the LORD, and in His law he meditates day and night. Psalm 1:1-2 NKJV

When you concentrate and think about God's Word, it is known as meditation. It just means you really focus on what God is saying, and think about how a verse speaks to your life. Is there a sin to confess? Is there a promise to claim? Is there an attitude to change? Is there a command to obey? Is there an example to follow? Is there a prayer to pray? Is there an error to avoid? Is there a truth to believe? Is there something to be thankful for?

Begin the practice of trying to think about God's Word as your last thought before you go to sleep and your first thought when you wake up and begin the day. When you find yourself concentrating on God's truth, you will find yourself being impacted and changed by God's truth.

Finally, there is one more thing you must do to really delight in God's truth.

APPLY GOD'S WORD TO YOUR LIFE

God does not give you His Word just to inform you, He gives you His Word to transform you. God isn't just trying to educate you; He is trying to change you. Your maturity is measured by your character and your conduct, not by your knowledge or what you say.

When God shows us truth in His Word, we need to apply it to our lives and live differently. That is what the "so what" questions lead you to. So what difference does this make in your life? So what are you going to do about it? So what are you going to change?

Can you imagine waking up in the morning, looking in the mirror first thing, and seeing a mess? Of course you can, we all do it every day. Now, imagine someone who looks in the mirror, sees a mess and then walks outside and goes on their way to school or work without doing anything about their appearance. God says that is what it is like to look into the Bible, see God's truth, and then keep living the same way.

Do not merely listen to the word, and so deceive yourselves. Do what it says. Anyone who listens to the word but does not do what it says is like a man who looks at his face in a mirror and, after looking at himself, goes away and immediately forgets what he looks like. But the man who looks intently into the perfect law that gives freedom, and continues to do this, not forgetting what he has heard, but doing it — he will be blessed in what he does. James 1:22-25 NIV

God's Word contains truth that is meant to affect the way we live. It is the standard that we go by. It is God's instruction manual for life. As you listen to God's word, read it, study it, memorize it, and think about it, let it sink in and transform the way you think and the way you see life. There is power in God's Word. There is no discipline in your spiritual life as important as this one. All the other disciplines spring from this: study God's Word, delight in God's truth.

When you accept God's Word as truth, hide it in your heart, and then apply it to your life, you are delighting in God's Word. You can't go deeper with God without doing that. You can't discover this dynamic life without doing that. But when you delight in God's truth, God begins transforming your heart, the way you think, the way you see the world, and you begin to discover what dynamic life is all about.

Growth Steps

Take these growth steps to discover dynamic life:

- Start reading the Bible every day. Set a time of 5-10 minutes to read a portion of the Bible.
- Develop a plan to read the Bible. Start with the passages listed below.
- Begin to keep a notebook where you can record your thoughts, questions, and application points.
- Purchase a good study Bible, and make sure you have a translation that is reliable and easy to read.
- If you have not already done so, join a Bible study group where you can study the Bible with others.
- Use the devotional guide below for this chapter and every chapter to begin the habit of reading the Bible and memorizing different verses.

Devotional Guide

Read through these passages over the next week and write your observations, questions, and applications to your life.

Monday:	2 Timothy 3:10-16
Tuesday:	2 Peter 1:16-20
Wednesday:	Acts 17:1-12
Thursday:	Nehemiah 8:1-12
Friday:	Matthew 4:1-11
Weekend:	2 Timothy 2:15-19; Psalm 128

This Week's Memory Verse

I have hidden your word in my heart that I might not sin against you. Psalm 119:11 NIV

Chapter Three

Yield Some Time to God
The Discipline of Praying

*Call to Me, and I will answer you, and show you great
and mighty things, which you do not know.*
Jeremiah 33:3 (NKJV)

TALK TIME

God wants to talk. Imagine it. The Creator of the universe really wants to spend time with you. He really wants to talk to you, and He really cares what you have to say.

When we talk to God, it is called prayer. Some people talk about prayer in such a way that you might actually feel discouraged to try. It kind of sounds like a super-spiritual religious act for mystics more than something that is practical and important for every Christian. You may have even tried to pray and found it dull and uninteresting. It isn't that you don't care; it is just that it seems so hard. Who wants to talk to themselves? And while you know God is out there, when He doesn't seem to answer back, well, it just takes the excitement out of it. And hey, God knows what is going on anyway. So many people just casually give up on prayer and practice it only in a very limited way.

But what if God really did want to talk to you? What if He really did listen and would respond based on what you asked? What if you could learn how to talk to God? And what if you could learn to discern His voice in your life?

Maybe the first step is realizing that prayer is not primarily about telling God anything, or getting anything from God. It isn't primarily a religious duty, and it certainly isn't about impressing anyone else. Prayer is about talking to God. That's it, pure and simple. It's about having conversations with God.

You can't build a strong relationship with someone without talking and listening, and you can't talk to someone if you don't invest the time. That is why the next step in your spiritual growth is to yield some time to God to talk and to listen.

Jesus' disciples knew they needed to learn how to have conversations with God and so they asked Him to teach them how.

> *Now it came to pass, as He was praying in a certain place, when He ceased, that one of His disciples said to Him, "Lord, teach us to pray…"* Luke 11:1 NKJV

Now think about that question. Of all the things they could have asked Jesus about, they asked about how to pray. Somehow they knew that the time Jesus spent with His Father was the key to everything else. They were right. You can't grow into dynamic life unless you spend some time with God and learn to talk.

Here are several key steps to learning to yield some time to God in your life.

BE AWARE OF GOD'S PRESENCE

It is easy to know when a friend or companion is present and available to talk. The phone rings and we hear their voice, they walk in the room with a smile and an outstretched hand, or they sit down at the table with a hot cup of coffee. It's time to talk. But with God it can seem more difficult, at least at first. How do we know that God is there? That He is ready to talk? Obviously, you need to develop a spiritual sense of God's presence.

The first thing you need to know is that God is always there. He is everywhere. Many verses confirm what theologians call the "omnipresence" of God.

- *"Am I a God who is only in one place?" asks the LORD. "Do they think I cannot see what they are doing? Can anyone hide from me? Am I not*

everywhere in all the heavens and earth?" asks the LORD.
Jeremiah 23:23-24 NLT

- *God did this so that men would seek him and perhaps reach out for him and find him, though he is not far from each one of us. "For in him we live and move and have our being."* Acts 17:27-28 NIV

- *Where can I go from your Spirit? Where can I flee from your presence? If I go up to the heavens, you are there; if I make my bed in the depths, you are there. If I rise on the wings of the dawn, if I settle on the far side of the sea, even there your hand will guide me, your right hand will hold me fast. If I say, "Surely the darkness will hide me and the light become night around me," even the darkness will not be dark to you; the night will shine like the day, for darkness is as light to you.* Psalm 139:7-12 NIV

Yet, just knowing that God is not limited by time or space hardly seems the same thing as sensing that God is near and ready to talk. God's omnipresence isn't the same thing as His intimacy. In order to have a close personal relationship with God, you need to understand some basic things about His nature. God is a Spirit, and His Spirit is called the Holy Spirit.

When Jesus left, the Holy Spirit descended and began to live within the hearts of those who were followers of Christ. Intimacy with God entered a whole new period. We sometimes think of Jesus as absent, since we can't see him in the physical realm, but in reality He is present, as real as ever. In fact He is more real than ever, through His Spirit. His Spirit is His presence. God is with us. God is with you.

Look at the following verses that concern the work of the Holy Spirit.

- *But the Counselor, the Holy Spirit, whom the Father will send in my name, will <u>teach you</u> all things and will <u>remind you</u> of everything I have said to you.* John 14:26 NIV

- *But when he, the Spirit of truth, comes, he will <u>guide you</u> into all truth. He will not speak on his own; <u>he will speak</u> only what he hears, and <u>he will tell</u> you what is yet to come. He will bring glory to me by taking from what is mine and <u>making it known</u> to you. All that belongs to the Father is mine. That is why I said the Spirit will take from what is mine and <u>make it known</u> to you. In a little while you will see me no more, and then after a little while you will see me.* John 16:13-16 NIV

Now go back and focus on every underlined word. They all point to the Holy Spirit speaking to or communicating with us. Again and again, Jesus promised that the Holy Spirit would come to speak to us. He used words like *guide, teach, tell,* and *makes it known,* but the point is the same. In the Holy Spirit, God is present to personally relate to us. Now, God may not speak verbally to you. Why should He? After all, why should He speak from the outside, when He already lives on the inside? Someone was asked, "Does God speak audibly to you?" The believer replied, "No, He speaks much louder than that!" The point is not the means by which God speaks or communicates, but that He does. Jesus said, *He who belongs to God hears what God says* (John 8:47 NIV).

If you want a conversation with God, begin by "practicing His presence." Realize that God is with you, around you, in you. Imagine Him walking with you, driving with you, at work beside you. See Him as a constant companion who desires to speak and to listen throughout the day. Determine to spend at least one day next week practicing His presence. Make yourself constantly aware throughout the day that God is with you. From the time you say, "Good morning" to Him at the start of the day until the time you say, "Good night" at the end, visualize His presence, sense His presence, and interact with Him all day long.

Prayer is not trying to rouse some slumbering deity far away. It is not trying to impress God with our piety or virtue; it is having a conversation with our friend who is as close to us as our next breath.

PLAN SOME TIME FOR GOD

The Bible says to *pray without ceasing.* Your communication with God should be constant. It doesn't just happen in a 15-minute pre-arranged time. However, we do need to schedule some time for God. Why? Because if we don't schedule some time then we're likely to drift and find that we aren't spending any time with God at all. It's just like a friendship. Have you noticed how busy life can be? Your good intentions to connect with a friend aren't enough. You have to put it on the calendar. You set a time and a place, especially when you are just starting to build the friendship.

The same thing is true with God. You need to set a time and place to connect with God on a regular basis. When God gave His ten commandments to His people, one of them dealt with keeping a day reserved for God. God said, *Remember the Sabbath day, to keep it holy* (Exodus 20:8 NIV).

God was reminding His people that they had six other days to work and do everything else they needed to do, but one day was to be reserved for worship and rest. It is important to continue the habit of worshipping God every weekend with other believers as a church. The weekly habit of giving that day to God to worship, as well as worshiping and resting from our normal activities will remain a key discipline in your spiritual health for the rest of your life.

Giving God a day a week is important, but you need more. If you truly want to build a strong relationship with God you need to give God some time every day. Jesus modeled spending time with God on a daily basis. Luke 5:16 says that Jesus would *withdraw to desolate places and pray* (ESV). And Mark 1:35 describes Jesus practice of *rising very early in the morning, while it was still dark, he departed and went out to a desolate place, and there he prayed* (ESV).

Your relationship with God must be something you pursue every day. That is why once a week isn't enough. You need God's direction daily. You need God's provision daily. You need God's protection daily. You need God's strength daily. You need God's wisdom daily. You need God's power daily. Get the point? We need to yield time to God everyday.

Here is what I recommend: Start by scheduling some time with God every day. It can be 15 minutes. If you have longer, you can work up to 30 minutes. The quality of time matters more than the quantity of time. Find something that can become a habit in your life that you can maintain over the rest of your life. I would rather you start with 10-15 minutes and learn to be consistent with that than try some long time frame like 30 minutes or longer and then have difficulty maintaining that. So the first step is set a time.

Next, set a place. Where can you meet with God with minimal or no interruptions? Hey, I know that can be really hard depending on your schedule and family situation, but it's important. Some people have a place in their home where they can get alone and be private with God. It may be an office or a patio. Bill Anderson was the pastor of Calvary Baptist Church in Clearwater for 27 years before I became the pastor. He became famous around our church for his "prayer bush." There was a large hedge-like bush at his house, and he literally kept a chair out there and would go sit and spend some time with God. It worked great until a policeman patrolling the neighborhood saw him sitting in the hedge at 5:00 in the morning and mistook him for a prowler. Hey, whatever works for you; just find your spot.

The next step is to have a plan. What are you going to do with your time with God? It can look a lot of different ways, and over time you'll learn to create a time with God that is uniquely yours. If you're just getting started, here is what I would suggest.

Start with prayer. Spend one or two minutes clearing your mind and heart and asking God to speak to you. Acknowledge that you need His help and guidance. Tell Him that you love Him and want to know Him better.

Read the Bible. In the last chapter we talked about the importance of reading and studying the Bible. This is where you do it. Spend five to ten minutes reading the Bible. Follow some type of reading plan like the ones I suggested in the last chapter. Read through a book of the Bible, study a topic in the Bible, or follow a devotional guide. As you get comfortable doing this you will learn to study the Bible more and more. You can begin to take notes and keep a journal. As you grow, this part of your time with God can grow longer and longer, but the important thing is that you are spending some time reading the Bible for yourself every day.

Pray. After your Bible reading time is done, spend the last 5-7 minutes in prayer. We'll look at some specific suggestions for how to talk with God later in this chapter. End your time with God praying for the things that are on your heart. Pray for other people. Pray for God's guidance through the day.

One of the advantages to spending time with God early in the day is that it helps you remain aware of His presence throughout the day. When you yield some time to God every day, it strengthens your relationship with Him and helps you experience dynamic life.

Keep a journal. One thing you should consider is keeping some kind of spiritual growth journal. It can be as simple as a plain notebook or as developed as a guide someone else has produced. A journal will help you write down thoughts from your Bible study, such as questions you have, conclusions you've drawn, and applications you want to make. It can also serve as a prayer journal to record requests you are praying for. It can be an exciting thing to specifically write down your prayer requests and then later go back and see how God really does answer prayer.

Now here are some random thoughts about planning time for God. Don't get on a guilt trip. This isn't meant to make your life harder, it is meant to make your life better. You may miss a couple of days or stumble at some point. Just get back at it. God loves you and wants to spend time with you, and you should view your time with God not as a legalistic obligation, but as an opportunity to know God better.

Don't worry about dry times. You may go through periods where prayer seems difficult or the Bible seems confusing. You may begin to wonder if it is worth it to keep going, or if it is even doing you any good. Habits can be hard to form, particularly when they are good for you and require discipline. Is exercising easy? Eating right? That is why they call it discipline. It can be hard. Trust me on this one. You need this time with God more than anything. Don't quit because you've failed; don't quit because you're discouraged. Don't ever quit. Keep trying, keep working, keep pressing, and soon you will form a habit of yielding time to God that becomes a part of your routine, a natural part of your life. When you do, you will be spiritually healthier.

Finally, let me say a word to those of you who have been followers of Christ for a long while. The idea of yielding time to God is nothing new. You've heard it before and some of you have tried it before. Maybe in your first years of spiritual growth you were enthused about this discipline and committed to it, but now you've slacked off. You read the Bible on occasion, still go to church, pray before meals, but you know your spiritual life isn't as vibrant as it could be or should be. You might even be looking for something new, some new experience, some new teaching, or some new spiritual insight that will jump start you spiritually and bring back your first love. When I talk about such simple things as yielding time to God, you are tempted to cruise on by because you've been there and done that. Can I say something to you? What you need is not something new, but something old. Sometimes the answers to our dilemmas are right in front of our faces. We already know what to do; we just aren't doing it. You may be tempted to blame a group, a church, a pastor, a spouse, or your old dog that is getting on your nerves, whatever. But in reality the problem of your spiritual dryness is as simple as your failure to put God first in your life, and it is seen in your unwillingness to yield some time to God every day in prayer and Bible Study.

Yield some time to God weekly and daily, and you will experience dynamic life. Now before we leave this topic let me share a few other insights that will help you learn to talk to God.

PREPARE YOUR HEART FOR GOD

The most famous teaching on prayer is found in Mathew 6:5-13. Verses 9-13 contain what is commonly called the Lord's Prayer. You've probably heard it, prayed it, or heard it prayed or quoted. In verses 5-8, Jesus actually talked about our attitude toward prayer. We have to prepare our hearts before we begin to talk to God. It isn't just what you say, but how you say it and why that is important. This is because many people have learned superstitions and formulas for prayer that have very little to do with really talking to God.

In the ancient world and in many religious traditions, people thought that they could manipulate God to get what they wanted by repeating certain words or phrases. You may have even learned to pray pre-written prayers believing they had more power and could evoke God to act. You can still see people today in certain faith traditions repeating phrases over and over as if believing that if they only said something enough times, then God would finally be pleased and respond to their prayers. Others pray in order to appear religious and impress others. Jesus countered these false ideas of prayer and taught us to pray in a natural authentic fashion. Notice what He said,

> *And when you pray, you must not be like the hypocrites. For they love to stand and pray in the synagogues and at the street corners, that they may be seen by others. Truly, I say to you, they have received their reward. But when you pray, go into your room and shut the door and pray to your Father who is in secret. And your Father who sees in secret will reward you. And when you pray, do not heap up empty phrases as the Gentiles do, for they think that they will be heard for their many words. Do not be like them, for your Father knows what you need before you ask him.* Matthew 6:5-8 ESV

Jesus seemed to be saying *get real.* He criticized those who prayed in public places so that others would be impressed. It isn't about what others think; it is about you and God. If you're more worried about what others think about you than what God knows about you, you are in real trouble. Prayer is about you and God. It is personal. Keep it real. He spoke of getting in a private place. Jesus said *shut the door* and *pray in secret.* Jesus was not condemning public prayers. After all, He prayed in public. Why else would the disciples have observed Him and asked Him about His prayer life? His point was that prayer is about your personal relationship with God, not impressing people with how religious you are. Your motives matter. Pray to know God. Pray to talk to God. If you only pray in public then something is wrong. You may pray in public, or pray out loud with others in a group, but the real purpose of prayer is to help you know and connect with God. Prayer should start in a private place, just you and God.

You can get real with God because He wants to get real with you. Who wants to go on a date with someone who pretends to be something they are not? Fancy formulas, big words, and religious jargon do not impress God. He loves you. You do not have to pretend with Him. He knows what you need. He knows what you feel. He knows where you are struggling. So why pretend? If you are frustrated, worried, anxious, angry, disappointed, happy, or sad, talk to God like you would a friend. Of course, we think of God in terms of reverence and holiness, as we should, but the more authentic and genuine your discussions with God are, the more powerful and meaningful your prayer life will be.

One of the good ways to learn how to pray authentically is to read through the book of Psalm. Many of the psalms are really prayers -- discussions with God. You will find every emotion—doubt, anger, sorrow, disappointment, joy, relief, and thanksgiving—in the psalms. Don't try to impress God and don't try to impress others. Be you. Be real. Talk to God. He wants a relationship with you, warts and all, not someone you pretend to be.

LEARN TO TALK TO GOD

So what do you say to God? What does God want to know from you? After Jesus said how NOT to pray, He then gave a model prayer. He gave us a guide on how to pray. Sadly, this model prayer, commonly called the Lord's Prayer, has itself been used as a "vain repetition," empty meaningless words repeated with a kind of superstitious hope. That is not what Jesus had in mind. The Lord's Prayer was given as an example to help us know how to pray. So that it sounds a little different than normal, look at it in the NLT:

> *Pray like this: Our Father in heaven, may your name be honored. May your kingdom come soon. May your will be done here on earth, just as it is in heaven. Give us our food for today, and forgive us our sins, just as we have forgiven those who have sinned against us. And don't let us yield to temptation, but deliver us from the evil one.* Matthew 6:9-13

How do we talk to God? First, *focus on Him.* Jesus started the prayer with the focus on God. He told us to pray that God's name is honored. That is always the best place to start your prayer, with the focus on God, not you. The Bible says,

> *Enter into His gates with <u>thanksgiving</u>, and into His courts with <u>praise</u>. Be thankful to Him, and bless His name.* Psalm 100:4 NKJV

Notice the two key words *praise* and *thanksgiving.* Those two words hold the key to be ushered into God's presence. How many of our prayers start with the focus on ourselves not God? Probably most of them. "God, I want this. God, I need this. God, please do this." Instead, start by focusing on God.

Thanksgiving is realizing what God has done and giving Him gratitude. Praise is recognizing who God is and giving Him glory (credit). Those two qualities help us focus on God and get our prayer started right. Start by being thankful. Think of things you are thankful for or should be thankful for and express your gratitude to God. Be thankful even if you just name one or two things. Start by being thankful. Then give Him praise. Think of some attribute of God, some descriptive phrase about His character or His power, and give God the credit. Praise Him. You know how to praise a child who does well. You know how to praise a friend who accomplishes something great. Praise God. There is no shortage of things to praise Him for. Start your prayer by focusing on God through thanksgiving and praise.

The second part of your prayer is to *focus on what God wants.* Usually we begin our prayers with what we want. Start with what God wants, what His will is. Jesus prayed, *May your will be done here on earth, just as it is in heaven.* Pray about what matters to God. Talk about His kingdom, His purposes. Find out what God cares about, and talk about those things. What matters most to God? Think about people coming to know Christ and pray for lost souls to be saved. Think about His church expanding, and pray that many come to Christ and are built up in the faith. Think about His concern for people. You can pray for peace and justice in the world. Just imagine what God's kingdom will look like when sin is abolished, violence ceases, and the knowledge of the glory of the Lord fills the earth. Learn what the Bible teaches about God's kingdom. Imagine what heaven will be like, and pray for God's will to be accomplished on the earth. By focusing on what God wants rather than what you want, you will learn what to pray for and your heart will grow to desire the things that God desires. This is what it really means to pray in Jesus' name, in His will. We desire that which God desires and it is the secret to powerful life-transforming prayer. Start with what God wants.

The next part of your prayer is to *focus on your needs.* The prayer for daily food is not just an empty phrase. It is a confession that all our blessings and our daily provisions to live come from God. Tell God what you need. There is a difference between what you want and what you need. Sometimes the line gets a little blurry, but try to focus more on needs than wants. Clearly, you need many things. You have physical needs like food and water. Even when you feel confident about where those are coming from, our prayer for daily provision is a confession of our dependency on God and a recognition that He provides all that we have. So yes, pray for all your physical needs.

You also have material needs. You need clothes and shelter of course, but think also of all the financial needs you have. You may need a car or a job. There are many things that you may need. You may even be worried. Tell God what you are worried about. The Bible says,

> *...do not be anxious about anything, but in everything by prayer and supplication with thanksgiving let your requests be made known to God.* [7] *And the peace of God, which surpasses all understanding, will guard your hearts and your minds in Christ Jesus.* Philippians 4:6-7 ESV

God cares about your needs. The Bible promises that God will provide for your needs (Philippians 4:19). Tell God what you need. Tell God what you are worried about.

Finally, *focus on your spiritual needs.* There are two spiritual needs Jesus mentioned in His model prayer. The first was forgiveness. Ask God for forgiveness. A Christian knows that God has already forgiven Him, but unconfessed sin hinders our relationship with God and harms us spiritually. A big part of your prayer is making sure things are right with God. Make sure you spend time confessing your sin to God and seeking His forgiveness. Confession should be a regular part of your prayer time.

You also need God to direct and steer your paths. Jesus taught us to pray for God's guidance away from temptation, to deliver us from evil. Ask for God's help for the day ahead. Ask Him to order your steps and direct your paths so that you can avoid the things that harm you and others. The Bible says,

Trust in the LORD with all your heart, and lean not on your own understanding; In all your ways acknowledge Him, and He shall direct your path. Proverbs 3:5-6 ESV

When you acknowledge God's authority, recognize the limits of your own wisdom, and ask for God's help, you can have confidence that God will direct your steps. You need His help. Ask for it.

When you pray, focus on God, on what He wants, and then focus on your needs, material and spiritual. That is how Jesus taught us to pray. Make a few minutes of prayer a key part of your time with God. But remember God wants to talk to you throughout the day. The Bible actually says to, *...pray without ceasing* (1 Thessalonians 5:17 NKJV).

Your daily time with God will form the foundation of your prayer life. But you can talk to God throughout the day. Remember His presence. Breathe a prayer to Him as you face difficult or stressful situations. Constantly ask for His help and direction. Thank Him throughout the day for His goodness and provision. Keep your conversation with God going on all the time.

Now, we talk to God in prayer, but does God speak to us? Can we hear the voice of God? Every relationship involves talking and listening. In the Bible, God promises that He will direct our paths, convict us of sin, comfort our hearts, and much more. What does it mean to hear God's voice and sense His direction?

LEARN TO LISTEN TO GOD

Most people don't hear God speak audibly. They don't hear an actual voice. Yes, there are times in the Bible when God spoke audibly, but they seem to be the exception not the rule. Yes, you will find people who tell of extraordinary circumstances when they claim to have heard an audible voice. I can't debate someone's experience, but I can assure you that the vast majority of the time when you hear someone talk about God speaking to them, they are not referring to an audible voice. You don't have to hear an audible voice to hear from God. After all, it just makes sense that if God is living on the inside of us, He doesn't need to climb outside of us to speak! Since God lives on the inside of our hearts, in our spirits, He speaks to us in our hearts, we sense Him in our spirit. So how do you hear His voice?

Henry Blackaby in his book *Experiencing God* observed that God speaks in a variety of ways.[7] He speaks first *through His Word.* This is the first place we learn to hear God's voice. When you read the Bible, you are hearing God's voice. Sometimes as you read the Bible a particular verse or truth just seems to jump out at you. It is amazing how often God will reveal a specific truth at just the time you need to hear it. This is one reason why reading the Bible and prayer go together. It is a way of talking to God and hearing from God at the same time. Always remember that when you do sense God speaking to you, it will be consistent with His Word if it is really His voice. God's voice in your heart will never contradict the revealed truth of the Bible.

God also speaks *through His Spirit.* As you talk to God and try to discern His voice, you may feel impressions or gain insight that comes from His Spirit inside of you. Sometimes it is just like a truth opens up before your eyes. At other times you feel a distinct prompting in your spirit. Many people have stories about how it just seemed like God

---

[7] Blackaby, Henry. *Experiencing God.* (Nashville: Broadman & Holman, 1988).

wanted them to go somewhere or say something to someone, only to find out later that it could only have been God directing their steps. You don't have to pretend or fake it, but be open to God's voice and it just may surprise you how clearly God can speak and how specifically He can direct your steps.

God also speaks *through other people* as godly people give us counsel or insight. There is wisdom to be found in others. When you have mature, strong believers in your life, God can work through them to make His will clear. As always, their advice needs to be measured against God's Word, but there is much to be gained from the insight of spiritual people God has put in your life.

Finally, God can also speak *through circumstances* as you see Him at work around you. When you've been faithful to read God's Word, pray, and listen to the counsel of others, sometimes you just see God's hand in events and circumstances that occur. It's amazing what happens when you open your spiritual eyes and your spiritual ears and just ask God to speak. He does. And the more you learn to listen to His voice, the more you cultivate your spiritual ears to hear. So take some time to listen. You may find that God is speaking louder and more often than you think.

Every relationship must be nurtured. It takes time, effort, and communication to get to know someone better. If you want to grow in your relationship with God, become aware of His presence, plan some time for God, prepare your heart, learn to talk to God, and then learn to listen to His voice. If you will begin (or renew) the habit of yielding some daily time to God, it will pay rich dividends in your life and help you grow toward the dynamic life God has for you.

Growth Steps

Take these growth steps to discover dynamic life:

- Schedule a time and place to meet with God every day. Put it on your appointment calendar. Work to make this a lasting habit in your life.
- In your time with God (devotional time) make sure you read the Bible every day.
- In your time with God make sure you spend a few minutes talking to God in prayer.
- Keep a spiritual growth journal where you can record some of the things you are praying for and any insights you have during prayer.
- Practice having conversations with God throughout the day.
- Listen for God's voice in the Bible, in the impressions of His Spirit, through other godly people, and even in the circumstances of life.

Devotional Guide

Read through these passages over the next week and write your observations, questions, and applications to your life.

Monday:	Philippians 4:4-9
Tuesday:	John 17:20-26
Wednesday:	Acts 12:5-17
Thursday:	Nehemiah 1:3-10
Friday:	James 5:13-18
Weekend:	John 17:1-19; Psalm 65:1-13

This Week's Memory Verse

Call to me and I will answer you and tell you great and unsearchable things you do not know. Jeremiah 33:3 NIV

Chapter Four

Nurture Authentic Community
The Discipline of Connecting with Others

For where two or three come together in my name,
there am I with them.
Matthew 18:20 NIV

On April 16, 2007, a terrible tragedy unfolded in Norris Hall at Virginia Tech University. Before the morning was through, the worst mass shooting in US history had unfolded. Quickly, investigators put the puzzle together, and what emerged was a dark tragic picture. The gunman was Seung-Hui Cho. He had first killed two people in a residence hall for students. Calmly, he then walked across campus, entered Norris Hall, and randomly began shooting innocent people for no apparent reason. Before it was over, 33 had died and at least 15 other people were injured, and the nation was stunned. Who could do such a thing? What made this young student snap and commit such a tragic crime? Slowly a profile began to emerge of a very disturbed young man. The most common description? He was a loner. Doesn't that often seem to be the case when you hear about someone who snaps and does an unthinkable act? When people are isolated from healthy relationships and withdrawn from a healthy community of friends, they are vulnerable and sometimes that vulnerability gives way to terribly foolish choices.[8]

Many people struggle with loneliness. Few commit tragic crimes, yet still there is suffering. Usually it is quiet, within, and unseen. Many assume or believe that there is no one who cares, even if there are people who really do.

You aren't made to be alone. The very first thing God ever said was NOT good was loneliness when He said *It is not good that man should be alone* (Genesis 2:18 NKJV),

God made us for community. That is why when Jesus left, He left the Church. The Church is not an organization, it is not a denomination, and it is not an institution, at least not primarily. It may express itself in those ways, but

---

[8] "Virginia Tech massacre," Wikipedia. http://en.wikipedia.org/wiki/Virginia_Tech_shootings (accessed 16 Dec. 2011).

primarily it is a community, a family, a living group of people who want to follow Jesus.

Look at the Acts 2 passage below and notice every phrase that is an expression of the community of those early believers.

> *And they continued steadfastly in the apostles' doctrine <u>and fellowship, in the breaking of bread</u>, and in prayers...Now all who believed <u>were together</u>, and had all things <u>in common</u>, and sold their possessions and goods, and <u>divided them among all, as anyone had need</u>. So continuing daily with <u>one accord</u> in the temple, and <u>breaking bread from house to house</u>, they ate their food with gladness and simplicity of heart...* Acts 2:42-47 NKJV

Did you notice that everything in this passage is about the group? It wasn't a report about what one individual did, but what a community of people experienced together. Twice it is mentioned that they ate together. Why? Sharing a meal together is what friends and families do. When you want to get to know someone better what do you do? You ask them out to eat. And when real friendships flourish sharing a lunch or a night out is one of the most natural and enjoyable things to do. As families some of our best memories are shared around a table.

It also says they took care of one another. They met each other's needs. They were in each other's homes. The picture painted is one of real community. Friendships were formed. Burdens were shared. Meals were taken. And out of these burgeoning friendships people learned how to walk with Jesus and discover the life He had for them. They didn't do it in isolation, and neither can you.

In order to grow, in order to discover dynamic life, you need to nurture authentic community. Now, for some people that is easy. It's almost second nature. It just happens, and they don't even think about it. But for other people, it just seems harder. They may struggle with loneliness and crave a few real friendships. Regardless of how many healthy friendships you have right now, there are four things you can do to cultivate healthy relationships that can help you grow.

GET IN A GROUP

People group. A few friends hang out together. People share common interests, pursue similar hobbies, or just have a chemistry that draws them together.

Look at our passage again in Acts 2. Notice this verse.

> *And day by day, <u>attending the temple together</u> and breaking bread <u>in their homes</u>, they received their food with glad and generous hearts,* Acts 2:46-47 ESV

Now, notice that there were two basic venues where these believers met. Two types of meetings helped them grow in godliness. First, there was the *temple*. The temple was big. Literally, thousands could gather in the temple courts, singing, offering sacrifices, listening to teachers, and engaging in public worship. This was the big crowd. You need a big crowd environment in worship.

Now, look at the phrase *in their homes*. This is the second environment. They met together in homes. Since only a few people could meet in most homes, this was a smaller group and a more intimate setting. This is the second environment that you need in which to grow, the small group environment.

Now, there are some things you can do best in a big crowd, and there are some things you can do best in a small crowd. For instance, I think singing is better in a big crowd.

It sounds better, usually is better and you don't even have to be able to sing well to sing along!

But I like praying better in a small crowd. It is more intimate and you can pray about personal needs and pray for other people by name. I think teaching can be great in a big crowd. A gifted teacher can speak to the crowd and lots of people can hear the Word of God at once. There is something emotional and powerful about that. But you can ask questions best in a small crowd. You can go deeper and learn more.

The key thing is that you need both environments, the big one and the small one. If you only have one crowd, you are only halfway there!

Now, I like to think of a small group this way; it is a place where you know people by name and they know yours. In the late 80s and early 90s there was a sitcom named "Cheers." It was about a group of people who gathered regularly in a bar. What people who are old enough to remember often recall is the theme song for the show. There was a line in that song that said, *You want to be where everybody knows your name.*

I think that song struck a chord because it is true. You do want to go where everyone know your name. When a friend calls your name it's the best sound in the world. I think that is because we are made for community. Deep down we hunger to be known and to know others. It is the way God made us. It is the way God made you.

In fact, have you ever noticed how many shows and movies are built around a group? It doesn't need to be spiritual, and often isn't, but it still shows that everyone longs for community. The sad thing is that for most people the kinds of groups pictured on TV and in movies are the closest they will ever get to real community. They are fake, superficial, and sometimes even harmful. But the church is supposed to be the real thing, the real community we need and crave.

I have a friend who talks about "2 a.m. friendships." He says that a "2 a.m. friend" is someone you could call at 2 a.m. if you had a crisis, and they wouldn't think you're crazy. It's a friendship where the investment has gone deep and the trust level is high. That list is usually pretty short, but we all need a few people on that list whether we ever call at 2 a.m. or not. Some friendships aren't even that deep and personal, but they can still be significant. The point is that God made you for relationships and a big part of discovering the dynamic life that God has for you will come through healthy relationships with other believers.

There are all kinds of groups because there are all kinds of people. Some groups form around a physical time and place. This group meets on a Sunday morning in a certain room, or that group meets in a home on a particular night. People come and connect because of the time or place.

Some groups form around a topic of study. People are interested in learning about something and that draws them together.

Some groups form around a common life stage, like young families, or empty nesters, or moms with preschoolers. People going through the same things in life share the same burdens, the same challenges, and they naturally build community and help each other.

Some groups form around an interest. People share a hobby together and they just naturally begin to hang out. In our church we have a group of motorcycle enthusiasts who meet together and share their passion for motorcycling even as they grow in their passion for God.

Some groups form around a ministry. People are serving together in an area, and they build a community and connection with each other.

Some groups happen organically; they just seem to happen without any work or effort. You connect with some friends and the next thing you know you're in a group. Sometimes it takes little effort and a little structure. Most churches have some environment where people can get into small groups. As you can see, there many different kinds of groups.

Here is the key point; you've got to connect with others in community in order to grow spiritually. There are just some things that can only be learned in that kind of environment. The Bible says,

> *And let us consider how we may spur one another on toward love and good deeds. Let us not give up meeting together, as some are in the habit of doing, but let us encourage one another — and all the more as you see the Day approaching.*
> Hebrews 10:24-25 NIV

The Bible says we need to meet together so that we can spur one another onward toward love and good deeds (dynamic life). I like to think that a Life Group is any group that is meeting regularly and doing four things.

First, there is Bible Study. If your group is really helping you grow in your spiritual life, then at some point you had to read and talk about the Bible. It may be a mature teacher that your group has gathered around, or it may be a video you are watching and discussing together. Some groups will read a book and break it down. Just make sure that you are going to THE book and learning what God says (His book is still the best) and discussing how it applies to your life. The best part about Bible Study in a small group is that you can discuss its meaning and ask questions. You can share application points and lessons learned.

Second, there is prayer. Your group should pray for each other and practice prayer together. The best place to learn how to pray is in a group where people pray.

Third, a group is a place where people are getting to know each other and building friendships. That seems obvious, but it is important not to forget. Sometimes people join Bible studies where a gifted teacher explains the Bible, but there is never any interaction between people. No relationships are formed and no real life is shared. It may be a great Bible study, but you still need an environment where you can really connect with others.

Finally, groups are made up of people who serve each other. They take care of each other's needs. They help out. Everyone will go through some tough spots eventually. When a group is really healthy, people can share their burdens and others come forward to help. Some of the greatest moments I have ever had as a pastor were witnessing ordinary people walk through some of life's most difficult moments with each other. I've seen situations where I honestly wondered how somebody could get through without the friendships they had made and the support they had received from a close group of friends.

Now, maybe you are already in a group like that. Good. Stay faithful and recommit yourself to that group. Maybe you are in a group that is doing some of those four things but not all of them. You don't need a new group, you just need to make sure your group adds something so it can be a healthy group that encourages each other toward dynamic life.

If you're not in a group that you feel is helping you grow toward dynamic life then find one. Ask God to show you the right one. Talk to friends or leaders in your church about ways you can find a group to connect with. And if all else fails, start one. Find a few friends and start meeting together and studying the Bible together. You don't have to be a teacher. It's never been easier to find resources to help you study the Bible and grow. A group of three meeting together at a coffee shop and studying the Bible can still be the catalyst for spiritual growth in your life. I don't care where you meet, when you meet, or what the structure looks like. Find some friends, crack open the book, talk about spiritual things, pray for each other, serve each other, and the next thing you know you're on the way.

FOCUS ON OTHERS

Nurturing authentic relationships means you have to care about more than yourself. The key to forming healthy friendships is to care about other people. Find out what matters to them. Find out what they are facing. What are their challenges? Their fears? Their victories? What's going on in their job? Their family? Get your eyes off of yourself and think about others.

I recently conducted the funeral for a man in our city named Bill Gilkey. He had been a prominent but well-loved lawyer for decades in our community. Bill was a great conversationalist who often would ask people to *sit down and tell me about your victories.* I thought that phrase taught volumes about why Bill was such a success professionally and relationally. He was always positive and upbeat, and he always kept the focus on others.

Have you ever been with someone who just wants to talk about themselves? Not much fun, is it? After a while it's hard to pretend to be interested. They just go on and on about what is happening in their life without a thought that they've become a total bore to everyone else. Don't be that person!

The way to have someone like you is to love them. Everyone likes someone who loves them. Loving another person means you care about what they want, what they need, what they like, and it becomes all about them, and not all about you.

You can adjust your focus by looking at two things. First, focus on the spiritual growth of others. Look at Hebrews 10:24-25 again, where it *says …spur one another on toward love and good deeds…* (NIV).

Notice something? The focus there isn't your spiritual growth; it is someone else's. You are supposed to help someone else grow. Now, you can't bear responsibility for their growth -- only they can do that -- but you do have a responsibility to help them. It's ironic, isn't it, that helping someone else grow is a key to growing yourself?

Another way to adjust your focus is to focus on the needs of others. Again, look at the verse in Hebrews 10, *...but let us encourage one another* (NIV).

We all have needs. There will be times in your life where you will need help. You will need encouragement, prayer support, someone to do a favor, or maybe just someone to listen. You need to think about who you can encourage. You need to think about who you can serve. Just do something for someone else. That is also why you need to be in a group, because that is where you find out who has needs and what you can do to help. When you look at someone else's spiritual growth and someone else's needs, it helps adjust your focus off of yourself and puts it on others.

It was President John F. Kennedy who made the famous statement, *Ask not what your country can do for you, but what you can do for your country.*[9] That statement represents a powerful call to a mature perspective in life. Can I tell you something that other people may be afraid to tell you? You focus too much on yourself. How do I know? Because I do, too. We all do. It's called selfishness, and we suffer from it. The Bible says,

> *Each of you should look not only to your own interests, but also to the interests of others. Your attitude should be the same as that of Christ Jesus.* Philippians 2:4-5 NIV

It's not that you are unimportant to God or others. You are important and you do matter, especially to God. But spiritual and relational maturity is achieved when you care about others more than yourself. Try it. Spend some time this week thinking more about the problems of others than

---

[9] "Inaugural Address of John F. Kennedy," Wikipedia. http://en.wikipedia.org/wiki/Inaugural_address_of_John_F._Kennedy (accessed 16 Dec. 2011).

you own. Celebrate their victories, and empathize with their defeats. Work hard to change your perspective from "me first" to "you first." In the next conversation you have today or tomorrow, try to intentionally keep the focus on the other person. Make sure you find out how they are doing and what is going on in their life. Find out about their family. What burdens are they carrying around? Start making a conscious effort to care about the interests of others. You'll be a lot more fun to hang around and you might just end up building healthier relationships.

FELLOWSHIP WITH OTHERS

There is something about sharing a meal with someone, isn't there? Aren't you glad to know eating is spiritual? It is. When we eat together we build friendships, the kind of friendships that can help us grow.

Now, you can't force a friendship. You can't walk up to someone and get in their space and demand a relationship. It will freak them out, and they will run in the other direction (if they're smart!). Friendships happen naturally. They aren't forced, they just form.

That is why a group is a great place to start. A group is a safe place to share limited information and see who you want to get to know better. Now, if you find that person or persons, great, you can go deeper and get closer. But if you don't, that's OK, too. Sometimes you have to wait. Sometimes it just takes longer. That is also why a group is good. While you're waiting for a deeper friendship, at least you have the group.

When you have a connection with someone, encourage it and see where it leads. Don't assume anything or presume anything. That is the best way to kill a budding friendship.

Fellowship is when we share our lives with people. It is a spiritual thing when families go out and eat together. It is a spiritual thing when a group hangs out after church or barbecues in the backyard. By the way, barbecue is always, and I do mean always, spiritual! Fellowship is when we are involved in one another's lives.

In fact, there are over 50 commands in the New Testament that end with *one another*. Here are just some of them: *teach one another* (Colossians 3:16); *love one another* (1 Thessalonians 4:9); *comfort one another* (1 Thessalonians 4:18); *greet one another* (1 Peter 5:14); *receive one another* (Romans 15:7); *admonish one another* (Romans 15:14); *wait on one another* (1 Corinthians 11:33); *serve one another* (Galatians 5:13-14); *forgive one another* (Ephesians 4:22).

Now that's just a few. There are over 50 of them. Each is a command for believers, and we cannot do that if we aren't involved in someone's life. A friend at church is someone you want to spend "non-church" time with, and you do. Cultivate the godly relationships in your life. Invest the time. Practice the gift of hospitality by using your home. Look for opportunities to practice the ministry of "hanging out." Dynamic life is as much caught as it is taught. Hang around godly people who love Jesus and are serious about growing in their faith, and you will catch plenty of spiritual lessons. Paul wrote in 1 Thessalonians 2:8-9,

We loved you so much that we were delighted to share with you not only the gospel of God but our lives as well, because you had become so dear to us. (NIV)

Notice what he said. He shared not just the message of the gospel but his very life. In order to grow you must share your life with others and allow them to share their lives with you.

PROTECT THE UNITY OF THE CHURCH

There is one final point to mention about nurturing authentic community, and it is found in Ephesians 4:2-3,

> *Be completely humble and gentle; be patient, bearing with one another in love. <u>Make every effort to keep the unity of the Spirit</u> through the bond of peace.* Ephesians 4:2-3 NIV)

There is one thing that will destroy community faster than anything else and damage the testimony of the church and even the reputation of the gospel. That is division. Look again at Ephesians 4:2-3, and notice the command, *Make every effort to keep the unity of the Spirit*. The Bible commands us to protect the unity of our church.

It is sad to realize that our spiritual enemy loves to sow discord and division among believers. Churches have been torn apart by disputes and arguments that should easily have been settled. Nothing can destroy authentic community quicker than allowing unhealthy and needless division to cause schisms and conflicts.

Paul was dealing with one such conflict when he wrote in Romans 14:19,

> *Let us therefore make every effort to do what leads to peace and to mutual edification. Do not destroy the work of God for the sake of food.* (NIV)

Paul was referring to a division that was caused by food. Some people had convictions about not eating certain things, and other believers didn't share those same personal convictions. Paul called those personal convictions *disputable matters* (Romans 14:1). In other words, while there are some core beliefs that every Christian should have, there are other beliefs and behaviors that we may disagree on. While there needs to be unity on the essential matters of our faith, there needs to be liberty on the non-essential matters of faith. Some things are just personal preference. They are not essential to the gospel. Don't let a disputable issue cause division and destroy the work of God.

Unity is important because it pleases God and gives us a powerful witness to the world. Disunity displeases God and destroys our reputation.

- *I am praying not only for these disciples but also for all who will ever believe in me because of their testimony. My prayer for all of them is that they will be one, just as you and I are one, Father — that just as you are in me and I am in you, so they will be in us, and the world will believe you sent me.* John 17:20-21 NLT

- *By this all men will know that you are my disciples, if you love one another.* John 13:35 NIV

- *Behold, how good and how pleasant it is for brethren to dwell together in unity!* Psalm 133:1 NKJV

What can you do as one person to protect the unity of the church? Be patient with other people. Avoid critical attitudes and a judgmental spirit when things don't go your way. God's Word warns us not to pass judgment on disputable matters. Remember, you don't have to render an opinion on everything. There is no perfect church, no perfect pastor, no perfect groups, and you aren't perfect either. Someone once said if you find a perfect church don't join it, because it won't be perfect after you get there! Accepting imperfection is part of bearing with one another, as Paul commands in Ephesians 4.

Another important thing you can do is handle conflict biblically. Jesus taught that if we have a problem with someone we should go directly to them, in private, in person, and talk it over (Matthew 18:15).

Most divisions that grow usually are the result of someone acting unbiblically in handling their conflict. They talk about it with other people, or maybe they never talk about it at all and just nurse an offended spirit. Both of those choices are wrong. If you've got a problem with someone, the responsibility is yours. Don't wait for them, don't hold a grudge, and don't talk to others about it. If you do, your response will violate what Jesus said, harm you spiritually, cause division in the church, and still not solve the problem.

Finally, to protect the unity of the church, refuse to gossip. Gossip is a sin and it has big consequences. The Bible has much to say about it.

- *A gossip betrays a confidence; so avoid a man who talks too much.* Proverbs 20:19 NIV

- *People with hate in their hearts may sound pleasant enough, but don't believe them. Though they pretend to be kind, their hearts are full of all kinds of evil.* Proverbs 26:24-25 NLT

- *With his mouth the godless destroys his neighbor,* Proverbs 11:9 NIV

- *Starting a quarrel is like breaching a dam; so drop the matter before a dispute breaks out.* Proverbs 17:14 NIV

Since unity is a key to our witness, you share the responsibility of protecting the unity of your church by avoiding a critical spirit, handling conflict like Jesus taught, and by refusing to gossip.

Christianity is a team sport. It isn't intended to be played, or lived, alone. Spiritual maturity is as much caught as it is taught. You need other people, and other people need you. So if you want dynamic life you need to nurture authentic relationships. You can do that by getting in a group, focusing on others, fellowshipping with others, and protectting the unity of the church. Do these things and you will help create an environment where you can grow and experience dynamic life.

Growth Steps
Take these growth steps to discover dynamic life:
- Get in a group. If you haven't already done so, take the first step to find a group you can connect with. Even if it seems awkward at first, don't be discouraged; find a group and connect.
- Find someone in your life to focus on this week. Find out something about them that you don't know. Find out if they have a need or a burden. Pray for them. Encourage them. Take a definite step to deepen the friendship by focusing on what they need.
- Share a meal with someone. Invite another family out to eat or to your home. Choose a person or a family that you haven't connected with before.

Devotional Guide
Read through these passages over the next week and write your observations, questions, and applications to your life.

Monday:	Romans 12:9-21
Tuesday:	1 Corinthians 13:1-13
Wednesday:	Ecclesiastes 4:9-12
Thursday:	Romans 14:1-13
Friday:	John 15:9-17
Weekend:	Psalm 133 and Romans 14:14-23

This Week's Memory Verse
For where two or three come together in my name, there am I with them. Matthew 18:20 NIV

Chapter Five

Actively Serve Others
The Discipline of Serving

For we are God's workmanship, created in Christ Jesus
to do good works, which God prepared in advance for us to do.
Ephesians 2:10 (NIV)

God has something for you to do. In fact, before you drew your first breath, took your first step, or uttered your first word, God had already planned you for His purpose. You were made to serve God. In fact, serving the purposes of God is the only thing that will bring true lasting fulfillment. Now you may have a lot of things on your "to do" list, but because this comes from God, isn't it time to move it to the top and get busy?

In fact, finding and fulfilling God's purpose for your life is an essential step in dynamic life. At first this seems counterintuitive. It is natural to think that happiness and fulfillment come from pursuing your own agenda. We want other people to serve us. Jesus' first followers struggled with the idea just like we do. In Mark 10, you can read a story of how the disciples got into a heated argument. They were jockeying for position in Christ's kingdom, like political officials trying to get elected. It was all about who could climb to the top and who could be served by others. But Jesus redefined greatness when He rebuked them by saying,

> *You know that in this world kings are tyrants, and officials lord it over the people beneath them. But among you it should be quite different. Whoever wants to be a leader among you must be your servant, and whoever wants to be first must be the slave of all. For even I, the Son of Man, came here not to be served but to serve others, and to give my life as a ransom for many.* Mark 10:42-45 NLT

Jesus challenged their perspective head on and turned their manmade definition of success upside down, or you could say, right side up. While the disciples were arguing about who should be the greatest, Jesus redefined leadership in terms of service. The way up is really down. If you want to be great in the kingdom of God, you must first become a servant. Bill Hybels called this "descending into greatness."[10]

So what are the steps to changing your thinking, finding the purpose God has for you, and making a difference in the lives of others? Let's take a look.

CHANGE YOUR PERSPECTIVE

The first step is that you must change your perspective. You have to accept Jesus' definition of greatness, quit living for other people to serve you, and accept that God wants you to serve them. This idea of living a selfless life is central to the gospel and to growing into spiritual maturity. It is what Jesus meant when He spoke of finding your life by losing it. You have to lose your life in a cause greater than your own selfish interests. You have to live for something bigger than yourself.

You need to change your perspective about life. In Luke 10:30-37, Jesus told a story to communicate about what it really means to love and serve someone else. It is known as the story of the Good Samaritan.

> *Jesus replied with an illustration: "A Jewish man was traveling on a trip from Jerusalem to Jericho, and he was attacked by bandits. They stripped him of his clothes and money, beat him up, and left him half dead beside the road. By chance a Jewish priest came along; but when he saw the man lying there, he crossed to the other side of the road and passed him by. A Temple assistant walked over and looked at him lying there, but he also passed by on the other side. Then a despised Samaritan came along, and when he saw the man, he felt deep pity.*

---

[10] Hybels, Bill and Rob Wilkins, *Descending into Greatness*. (Grand Rapids: Zondervan Publishing House, 1993).

Kneeling beside him, the Samaritan soothed his wounds with medicine and bandaged them. Then he put the man on his own donkey and took him to an inn, where he took care of him. The next day he handed the innkeeper two pieces of silver and told him to take care of the man. 'If his bill runs higher than that,' he said, 'I'll pay the difference the next time I am here.'" "Now which of these three would you say was a neighbor to the man who was attacked by bandits?" Jesus asked. The man replied, "The one who showed him mercy." Then Jesus said, "Yes, now go and do the same."* Luke 10:30-37 NLT

The story is so powerful because the truth is so obvious. The first two men appeared to be religious. They had a profession but no practice. Who knows what their excuses were. You can always find an excuse not to serve. But the third man, the Samaritan, truly served, met the need, and made the difference. At the end Jesus' command could not be clearer, *Yes, now go and do the same.*

There are three things a servant is always willing to do. First, *they look*. They pay attention. The first two men saw the need but quickly averted their eyes and passed by. It was the last man, the servant, who saw the need and allowed it sink in.

Needs are all around us. You don't have to travel to the ends of the earth to find a mission field. It starts at your front door. Now, to really pay attention you have to be willing to do something that most of us aren't willing to do: allow interruptions.

I hate interruptions. I operate best on a schedule with a clearly defined goal that occupies my focus and my energy. But sometimes interruptions represent opportunities. Most of us miss the opportunities because we don't tolerate interruptions. The wounded man in Jesus' story was clearly an interruption to the Samaritan's schedule, yet he stopped what he was doing, adjusted his schedule, and took time to meet a need. Can I be honest with you? You will never develop a Christlike heart for service until you allow God to break into your schedule once in a while. What are you willing to change, or to adjust, so that God can use you to accomplish His purpose?

The second thing a servant does is *they act*. We've all had good intentions. But good intentions don't make a difference in anyone's life. The Samaritan did something. He stopped his horse, knelt beside the wounded man, mended his wounds, and took him to the inn to recuperate. You can say you love someone all you want to, but real love is proved by actions.

Finally, we see this quality in all servants: *they give*. In the end, the Samaritan was willing to give. He gave his time to help. He gave his money to pay the bill. There are a lot of ways to give. You can give your time. You can give from your talents and abilities. You can give your treasure, your money. You will need to learn all three types of giving if you really want to be a servant.

If you look at this story you will see three kinds of people. There are the *takers*, the thieves who took money from someone else. Then, there are the *hoarders*, the first two men who had resources but wouldn't share. Lastly, you see the *giver*, the Good Samaritan. Which one are you? The first attitude is, "What's yours is mine, I'll take it." The second attitude is, "What's mine is mine, and I'll keep it." The third attitude is, "What's mine is yours, and I'll give it." Remember, love always costs something. Servants develop a generous spirit; they aren't afraid to give.

Jesus redefined greatness. We have to learn to embrace His definition of success by changing our perspectives on life. The way up is to serve others. The way to happiness is to get your eyes off of yourself. The way to fulfillment is to help someone else.

You also need to change your perspective about ministry. When people get involved in churches and in ministry, they often develop a selfish attitude even in regard to spiritual things. We begin to think that ministry is about others serving us, and churches are filled with people who grumble if the music doesn't appeal to them, if the service times aren't convenient, or if something doesn't suit them exactly right. Since when did church become about other people serving us? I have been a pastor for a long time, and I have noticed that the happiest people are always those who are busy making other people happy.

Another false view of ministry is that it is something that only professionals can do. Many people think that you pay a pastor and staff so that they can do the work of ministry and the job of the "average" Christian is to come and enjoy the ministry of others. Actually this model has nothing to do with the church of the New Testament. Many Christians need to completely overhaul their view of ministry. Instead of looking to leaders to do the work of ministry, you need to see that the role of leaders is to prepare you to do the work of ministry. Look at what the Bible says,

> *It was he who gave some to be apostles, some to be prophets, some to be evangelists, and some to be pastors and teachers, to prepare God's people for works of service, so that the body of Christ may be built up...* Ephesians 4:11-12 NIV

God calls and gifts some people to be leaders, apostles, prophets, evangelists, pastors and teachers. The purpose of leaders is not to do all the work, the purpose of leaders is to prepare other people to do all the work. Can you imagine a football team taking the field and then asking their coaches to play the game? Honestly, can you see a bunch of middle-aged guys, way past their prime, trotting onto the field to play outnumbered against a team of young well-trained athletes? It would be a slaughter. The job of a coach is to prepare a team to play. Every team needs coaches. They understand the game, have more experience, and possess the wisdom and skill to prepare younger players to perform at their peak. Coaches prepare players, but players make plays. It takes players to play and win the game. Or can you imagine an army that only sends the generals out to fight? Yet this is exactly what is happening in most churches when people come to church and expect the pastors and key leaders to do all the ministry while they pray for them and support them financially. No wonder so many churches are anemic. We need to see the true role of leaders. If you want to change your perspective on ministry, then change your perspective on leaders from "serve me" to "equip me." Understand that God wants you to be a minister and that the job of your pastors and spiritual leaders is to help prepare you to do what God wants you to do.

You also need to change your perspective on membership. The point of belonging to a church is not so other people can serve you, but so that you can learn to serve others. You need to change your view from "serve us" to service. In the Bible every Christian is called into full-time ministry. You may not work vocationally at a church, but you are called to serve God just the same. Don't think that vocational ministry is for those who get really serious about their faith. That is not true. Of course leaders should be serious about their faith. But some of the greatest spiritual champions in God's kingdom will never serve as pastors, but they are living out their faith and fulfilling their ministry. The idea that leaders serve and do ministry while members just attend church is killing our churches and rendering them impotent. Everyone is supposed to serve. God has something for you to do.

You also need to change your perspective on God. Instead of praying, "God bless me," our prayer needs to be "God, use me." Of course there is nothing wrong with seeking God's blessing, but if our greatest desire is always to enjoy the blessings of God without serving the purposes of God, then we are bound to be disappointed. And there are plenty of disappointed people sitting in churches every weekend. The blessings of God are found in the service of God. When you begin to care about what God cares about and begin to serve His purposes, you will find immeasurable blessings all along the way. Make your greatest prayer, "God, use me," and see if He doesn't answer that prayer and then bless you all along the way.

My friend Will Mancini is an author, ministry consultant and speaker. Will taught me that every Christian needs two "aha" moments. Do you know what an "aha" moment is? An "aha" moment is when the light bulb comes on and you get it. Suddenly you think, "Aha! I get it now." You need the first "aha" moment that realizes, "This is just for me." You come to the right church, understand the gospel, and trust in God and you realize, "This is just for me." You get it. The light bulb clicks on and you know, "This church, this message, God's love, it's for me." I hope you have that moment when you realize God's incredible love for you, and you see His providential plan for you in just the right place at just the right time. But you need another moment, another "aha."

The second moment is when you realize, "This is NOT just for me." It is when you realize that God brought you here not only to bless you but also to use you. God works in you so that He can work through you. He saved you to serve Him. He works in your life so that He can work through your life to touch others and expand His kingdom. It's how God works. He works through changed lives.

This is the first step toward actively serving others. You change your perspective about life and about ministry. You realize that it isn't about you, but that God made you and saved you for His purposes. Once you change your perspective then you are ready for the next step, which is to discover how God has uniquely shaped you for ministry.

DISCOVER YOUR *SHAPE*

How do you know where God wants you to serve? In most churches there are many opportunities to get involved, and there is no shortage of organizations looking for volunteers to help in some worthy cause. But the Bible indicates that God has something special for you to do. In Ephesians 2:10, God reveals *For we are God's workman-ship, created in Christ Jesus to do good works...* (NIV)

The word for "workmanship" is the Greek word *poiema*, from which we get our word *poem*. Just like a poet puts words together to say a certain thing, to sound a certain way, or touch a certain emotion, God also has created us, crafted us, to fulfill a particular purpose. We are God's poem. One translator (JB) says we are God's *work of art*.

You may not feel like a work of art, but you are. God made you and shaped you in a specific way and for a specific reason. God has something for you to do, and if you want to find out what it is, look at how He made you.

Rick Warren, pastor and author of *The Purpose Driven Life*, has popularized an acrostic to help us understand how God has shaped us for a purpose. Each person has a S.H.A.P.E. Your SHAPE is composed of five things that, put together, make you absolutely unique.[11]

S- Spiritual Gifts

A spiritual gift is a talent or ability that God has given you to accomplish His purpose. The Bible says, *But*

---

[11] Warren, Rick, *The Purpose-Driven Life*. (Grand Rapids: Zondervan, 2002).

each one has his own gift from God, one in this manner and another in that (1 Corinthians 7:7 NKJV).

The Bible lists many spiritual gifts, but there is no one list that is exactly the same as another. Most likely you have 2-3 primary gifts that God has given you to serve. The lists of some of those gifts can be found in Romans 12:6-8, 1 Corinthians 12:8-10, 1 Corinthians 12:28-30, and Ephesians 4:11. There are a variety of opinions about what some of those gifts are and the best way to use those gifts. Here are some things to remember. Everyone has spiritual gifts. Everyone is gifted, and that means you. It may take you a while to find those gifts, but they are there.

Everyone has different gifts. There is no single gift that marks spiritual maturity or the presence of the Holy Spirit. People have different gifts. Don't expect someone to look just like you, and don't try to mimic someone else's gifts just because you want to be like them. Gifts are in you. It's about finding out what they are and then developing those gifts to the fullest.

Also remember that your gifts aren't just for you, they are for the body of Christ, the Church. God has gifted you to bless others, so always remember your gift is to be used to help others grow spiritually. The best way to discover your gifts is to get busy serving. When you begin to actively serve others, your gifts will naturally rise to the surface. You will discover that you are good at certain things. You will begin to see the ways in which God has gifted you to bless others. Don't worry if you don't know right away. If you start serving, your gifts will become apparent.

H- Heart

You have certain things that you are passionate

about. Certain subjects grab your attention and motivate you to act, while other things bore you. The same thing is true for everyone. God created you to be you for a reason. Not everyone can care about the same things equally. One person is motivated to work with people, while others are motivated to work with numbers and raw data. Some people like working with their hands, making things out of wood, or fixing machinery. We're all different and that is OK. In fact, it is more than OK, it is the way God intended it. Don't worry that you aren't like somebody else. Be who God made you to be. What do you care about? What do you get angry about? What grabs your attention and won't let go? Your most effective ministry will flow out of your greatest passions.

A- Abilities.

There are some things you are good at. You need to realize that you can't divide your abilities into the spiritual, things God can use, and the secular, things that have nothing to do with God. Every ability you have comes from God, and He wants to use it for His purpose. Don't pretend you aren't good at something. That isn't humility, it is heresy. Remember, you are God's poem, God's masterpiece! How do you assess your abilities? First, look at your vocation. What do you do for a living? What talents do you need and use to be a success? Most people gravitate naturally toward things they do well. You can also look at your victories. Look in your past and ask yourself where you have succeeded. What have you done well? Find those areas and realize God has given you those abilities for a reason, and every ability, no matter how "un-spiritual" it may seem, is there for a reason. God can use it.

P- Personality

Various authors have written about some basic personality types. For instance, some people are direct, active and decisive. They are motivated by goals and results. Other people are outgoing, friendly, and enthusiastic. They are more motivated by relationships and personal inter-action. Still other people are detailed, cautious and highly analytical. Those people like routines, guidelines and ensuring things are done correctly. Another personality type is cooperative and supportive, and these people are moti-vated by harmony and peace.

Now, every personality type comes from God. Whether you're loud or quiet, whether you move quickly or deliberatively, or whether you like being around lots of people or prefer more solitude. Your personality comes from God and is part of His plan for your life. God uses different personalities to accomplish different things.

E- Experiences

You have certain experiences in life that have shaped you and formed you. They are your frame of reference. They affect how you see the world and view other people. For instance, look at your family background. Whether your family was healthy or dysfunctional, it has affected you. How about educational experiences? What have you learned and where did you learn it? Some of us learned the most in the school of "hard knocks"! Then there are your spiritual experiences -- times you met with God and heard His voice, or even your ministry experiences where you've served Him in the past. Sometimes our most powerful experiences are our painful experiences. Where have you been hurt? Where are the hidden scars? God never wastes a hurt. God is not the author of evil, but He can use any experience, no matter how bad it may be, to end up accomplishing His purpose in our lives. Often your greatest ministry flows out of your greatest hurt.

When you take those five characteristics and put them together, you discover a unique personal shape that will help determine your ministry. Your form determines your function. God would not give you certain characteristics, abilities, or experiences and then waste them. The Bible says, *But in fact God has arranged the parts in the body, every one of them, just as he wanted them to be* (1 Corinthians 12:18 NIV).

You are who you are for a reason. God has a special place for you to serve. While you should be willing to serve anywhere, just as an act of compassion and kindness, ultimately you need to find that special place of service that fits your shape. When you find it, you'll experience fulfillment and fruitfulness. It will feel just right because it will be, and you'll make the biggest difference in serving others. Now you are ready to make a difference.

MAKE A DIFFERENCE

When the late Steve Jobs wanted to encourage his employees at Apple to do great things, he would often exhort them to *put a dent in the universe*. It was his way of saying that he wanted to make a real difference.[12] You can make a difference. You can change the world. When you change the world for somebody else, you have made a difference and you have changed the world. When you make a difference for Christ you change the world in ways far more profound than inventing the latest technological gadgetry; you make a difference for eternity. There are

---

[12] Isaacson, Walter, *Steve Jobs*. (New York, New York: Simon & Schuster, 2011), 161.

several keys to making the biggest impact with your life.

First, you have to find your place. Where are you going to serve? We've already talked about discovering your SHAPE and how your form determines your function, but where do you find that function? Start first with your local church. I truly believe that the greatest impact you can have with your life is when you serve in and through a local body of believers, a local church. Look at what the Bible says in Romans 12:5, *So in Christ we who are many form one body, and each member belongs to all the others* (NIV).

You are part of the body of Christ. You belong to the rest of the body. You are one part of a greater whole. There are a lot of good organizations, but there is only one that is going to last forever, and that is the church of Jesus Christ. The Church is called the body of Christ and it is called the Bride of Christ. Your ministry should flow out of your connection and involvement in your local church. It is the best place to be accountable to others. It is the best place to be involved in something that will outlast you and will, in fact, last into eternity. It is the best place to contribute to the ministry of making Christ known around the world. It is the best place to continue growing spiritually.

In the Bible, Christ's followers did not act in isolation. They did not start ministries on their own, named after themselves, independent of the churches that they were part of. They worked in unison with other believers, and they always resulted in churches growing and expanding. I'm not against other organizations and charities. I just think that for a follower of Christ, your ministry should begin in your church and then grow from there. That keeps you connected with others, it keeps you under spiritual authority, it keeps you grounded in solid doctrine, and it keeps you focused on the advance of the gospel in your local community and around the world. If God expands your ministry beyond your local church, great — but let it start there. Look for what you can do to support the testimony of your church and expand the influence of your church.

Once you decide to serve Christ as part of your local church, you still have to decide where to begin. It's as simple as this: meet a need. Ministry is simply meeting needs in the name and power of Christ. Here is the secret. You serve God by serving people. Look for a need in a person's life and then meet it. The Bible says, *God has given each of you a gift from his great variety of spiritual gifts. Use them well to serve one another* (1 Peter 4:10 NLT).

Where do you start? Look at the *opportunities.* Usually if you just pay attention you will hear people asking for help. In most churches there are always numerous calls for help. Instead of just waiting for some perfect ministry to come along, why not get started by meeting an obvious need? God can steer a moving car better than a parked car. Get involved. Start serving somewhere, anywhere, and even if it isn't the perfect place for you to serve, you will be one big step closer to finding that place. You also need to understand that while there may be one major area for you to serve where you are perfectly shaped, there are always areas where you can lend a helping hand. You don't need any particular gift set to just stack chairs or help pick up after an event. Where there is an opportunity to serve, serve. Like the Nike slogan says, *Just Do It®.*

Look at the *problems.* Because of the way you are shaped, you will see problems that other people just won't see. That is good. There are always problems. There are always things that can be done better. You see them because you are shaped to see them. Now most churches or organizations don't need more problem spotters, they need problem solvers. Learn to be a problem solver. If you see a better way to do something, volunteer to help. If you are going to be vocal enough to point something out, then be willing to help solve the problem. Every problem is an opportunity for someone to serve.

Look at the *interruptions.* Interruptions can be your

greatest invitations to ministry. Remember the story of the Good Samaritan? Is there any doubt that he had not planned to care for a victim on the day he found the man on the side of the road? It was not in his schedule, but it was a divine appointment nonetheless. Just stay open. Don't become so goal oriented that you forget to see people who have needs and problems that are around you every day. You don't need a church ministry to touch somebody's life. Be the church. Be the ministry. Just take the initiative, serve, give, and do it in the name of Christ. When you do that, your church is ministering. One lady came to her pastor and complained about the church not doing enough for needy people. She told how she had seen someone the night before, bought them a meal, found them a place to stay, and just tried to help them in Jesus name. She asked, "Why doesn't the church do something for people like that?" The pastor responded, "It sounds like the church just did." She was the church. She was the minister, and she made a difference.

Look at your *friendships*. If you are still stuck and don't know where to get started, just look at some of your close friends in the church. Ask them where they are serving and just start helping. It is fun to serve alongside people you already know and like.

The key is to get started. Don't wait for the perfect situation. Don't expect your pastor or spiritual leader to know exactly where you are supposed to serve. They aren't the Holy Spirit. Start serving. Soon you will discover your gifts. Your SHAPE will become clearer, and if you stay open to God's leading you will soon find the perfect place to serve in your church and make a difference in someone's life.

The purpose of ministry is to help others. You are not only meeting needs, you are helping others grow (1 Corinthians 14:12).

Ministry is about helping other people grow. It is about building up the church and discovering in the process that you are growing. Focus on lifting up others and you will find that God is lifting you up. When someone laments they just aren't getting anything out of it … out of life … out of the church … out of the message … out of a friendship, maybe it is because they are looking at it all wrong. Instead of trying to get the most out of life, maybe we should be trying to add the most to it. As long as your perspective is self-centered, your spiritual life will not be dynamic. Focus on serving others and helping them grow, and watch your spiritual life come alive with dynamic power.

The secret to J.O.Y. is to understand the order of life. Jesus. Others. You. When you get those priorities in the right order, you will find joy. You won't find the dynamic life Jesus intended for you to have by focusing on yourself. You won't find real joy by living a self-centered life. Real life comes when you give your life to help others.

Growth Steps

Take these growth steps to discover dynamic life:

- Identify a need or a problem that needs to be corrected. It can be among your friends, in your church, or in your broader community. Think about what needs to be done to solve the problem and ask God if you are supposed to be part of the solution.
- Read through the lists of spiritual gifts in the Bible. Those lists are identified in this chapter. What gifts make sense to you and what gifts do not make sense? What do you think are the top two or three gifts that you have?
- Identify three things that you are really passionate about. Why do you think God gave you those passions? How can those passions be used to serve others?
- Recognize that all of your abilities come from God. Ask God to show you how you can use your abilities to serve His purposes. Tell God that your life belongs

to Him and that you are willing to be used by Him to
serve others and advance His kingdom.
- If you are not already involved in a ministry, get
  involved. Start by praying and looking for a place to
  start serving. Get going.

Devotional Guide
Read through these passages over the next week and
write your observations, questions, and applications to your
life.

Monday:	Philippians 2:1-11
Tuesday:	John 13:1-17
Wednesday:	Ephesians 4:11-16
Thursday:	Exodus 31:1-11
Friday:	Matthew 25:31-46
Weekend:	Psalm 139; Ephesians 2:1-10

This Week's Memory Verse
*For we are God's workmanship, created in Christ Jesus to do
good works, which God prepared in advance for us to do.*
Ephesians 2:10 NIV

Chapter Six

Magnify God with Passion
The Discipline of Worship

*You are worthy, our Lord and God, to receive glory and honor
and power, for you created all things, and by your will
they were created and have their being.*
Revelation 4:11 (NIV)

LEARNING TO LOVE

What is your favorite band? What is the best concert you ever attended? Are you a sports fan? Have you ever been to a packed stadium and seen the fanatics (that is where the word "fan" comes from) cheering their team? The truth is a great concert or a rocking sports venue is very much like a worship service. Songs are sung, praises are uttered, and incredible emotional displays of thanks can be rendered after a favorite song or an incredible play.

I will spare you my stories, because you probably have your own. If you do, you know there is something very special about being caught up in a crowd that expresses praise and thanksgiving. It is almost as if it is inside us, the need to worship, the need to praise. It is as if we are looking for something to be caught up in, something bigger than ourselves. While sporting events and concerts can be great events to attend, there is something sad about knowing that for many people that is the closest they will ever get to real worship. After all, at their best, other people do not deserve our worship. They may deserve gratitude, applause, and enthusiastic support perhaps, but worship? No way. However, there is someone who is worthy of our greatest worship and it should be reserved for Him alone.

When Jesus was asked what was the most important command in the Bible. He quoted from the Old Testament, Deuteronomy 6:4-5.

Hear, O Israel: The LORD our God, the LORD is one. Love the LORD your God with all your heart and with all your soul and with all your strength. Deuteronomy 6:4-5 NIV

This was the most basic confession a Jewish believer could make, and according to Jesus it summarizes everything in the Old Testament scriptures. What is the command? Love God. Worship is learning to love God and to love Him with all our heart, soul and strength.

You were made for God. When He created and shaped you, He made you to be in relationship with Him. Worship is our response to God's love. It is not a grudging, unwilling sacrifice. If it is, then it is not worship. Worship is seeing how good God is and realizing how much He has done for you. We then respond by giving ourselves back to Him, because that is the only reasonable thing to do (Romans 12:1-2).

Worship is about seeing God and then responding. It is knowing His greatness and His goodness, and then responding accordingly. We view the mercies of God, draw into His presence, and then we offer ourselves to Him.

The next component of Dynamic Life is to *Magnify God with Passion.* You must learn to worship God. Learn to cultivate a heart of genuine passionate worship.

VIEW GOD'S MERCY

People do not worship God because they do not know God. People are not motivated to worship God because they do not appreciate the mercy of God. If we see how wonderful God is, we cannot help ourselves. We will want to worship Him. You need to look at two things to appreciate how wonderful God is.

The first thing you need to see about God is how great He is. Look again at the verse in Deuteronomy 6:4-5 that Jesus quoted. Before the command was given to love God, notice that there was an affirmation of who God is. The Lord our God is one. Now, maybe that does not seem like a big deal to you, but the concept of the "oneness" of God was revolutionary. You see, most people on the earth knew there was a spiritual realm, but they did not understand it. Out of fear, ignorance, and superstition they imagined many different gods, deeply flawed, but who were somehow responsible for the entire created world and who could explain the mysteries of life. These pagan gods were thought to be responsible for the rain, sun, lightning, water, and everything in existence. The scarcity of water or blazing heat could be explained by a certain god's weakness, anger, or ineffectiveness. This superstitious view of life gave rise to ignorance and even wickedness, and weak gods were placated through violence or immorality. In essence, people on the earth simply projected their own strengths and weaknesses onto make-believe deities and really just worshipped themselves.

Against that backdrop of deception, ignorance, and unbelief, God revealed the truth about Himself. There is only one God. He is the Creator of all. Notice how often the concept of God as Creator is connected with the idea that He deserves to be worshiped.

- *For you created my inmost being; you knit me to-together in my mother's womb. I praise you because I am fearfully and wonderfully made; your works are wonderful, I know that full well.* Psalm 139:13-14 NIV

- *You created north and south. Mount Tabor and Mount Hermon praise your name.* Psalm 89:12 NLT

- *Let them praise the name of the LORD, for he commanded and they were created.* Psalm 148:5 NIV

- *They exchanged the truth of God for a lie, and worshiped and served created things rather than the Creator — who is forever praised. Amen.* Romans 1:25 NIV

- *You are worthy, our Lord and God, to receive glory and honor and power, for you created all things, and by your will they were created and have their being.* Revelation 4:11 NIV

If understanding God as Creator provokes a response of worship, is it any wonder why the doctrine of creation has been attacked so ferociously? How many people fail to worship God because their minds have been darkened by the lie that life itself can be explained apart from God? What would their response be if they truly saw that despite all attempts to the contrary, naturalistic evolution still has no explanation for the origin or complexity of life? God is the Creator and He deserves to be worshipped.

He is also perfect in character. He is mighty, and eternal. When you look at God's character throughout the Bible, you see He is all-powerful; there is nothing God cannot accomplish. Theologians call that the omnipotence of God. He is also everywhere; there is nowhere you can go to escape His presence. Theologians call that the omnipresence of God. He knows everything. There is nothing about you God does not know and nothing that will ever surprise God. Theologians call that the omniscience of God. God is omnipotent, omniscient, and omnipresent. He is simply the greatest and most powerful Being in the universe. He is the Creator and ruler of all, and the more you contemplate the greatness of God, the more awestruck you will be. He alone deserves to be called "awesome."

The more we reflect on His character and greatness, the more we are awed and moved to worship. The great hymn "How Great Thou Art" says it best,

Oh Lord my God, when I in awesome wonder
Consider all the worlds Thy hands have made,
I see the stars, I hear the rolling thunder,
Thy power throughout the universe displayed.

Then sings my soul, my Savior God, to Thee;
How great Thou art, How great Thou art!
Then sings my soul, my Savior God, to Thee;
How great Thou art, how great Thou art.[13]

It is the view of God's *mercy* that moves us to worship. While the first part of that is realizing God's greatness, the second part is realizing His goodness. His mercy is His love and affection toward us. What really moves us to passionate worship is that we realize that even though God is perfect and powerful, He knows us and cares about us.

God is great but we are not. We are not all powerful, we do not know everything, and we certainly are limited by time and space. Even more importantly, we are not great on the inside. In fact, the Bible says we have sinned. We are guilty of violating God's character and God's laws. We deserve complete separation from God, which means death, both physical and spiritual. That is what we deserve, but that is not what God offers us.

The greatest act of goodness is that God sent Jesus into the world to die for your sins. The Bible says,

He saved us, not because of righteous things we had done, but because of his mercy. He saved us through the washing of rebirth and renewal by the Holy Spirit,

---

[13] Boberg, Carl. "How Great Though Art," trans. Stuart K. Hine. Music by (Kingsway: Kingsway Communications Ltd., 1953).

whom he poured out on us generously through Jesus Christ our Savior. Titus 3:5-7 NIV

When we think of God's mercy toward us, it moves us to passionate worship. We are not religious types who are puffed up with self-righteous pride simply trudging through the motions of thanksgiving and praise. We are sinners plucked from the fires of hell who have been given life when we did not deserve it. We have been given forgiveness when we could not earn it. We are children of the Most High God, and we have the certainty of eternal life. No wonder we want to applaud Him. No wonder we want to sing His praises. In view of God's mercy, we worship. Consider the words of James Huey in this worship song,

> *When I think about the Lord*
> *how He saved me, how He raised me*
> *how He filled me with the Holy Ghost*
> *how He healed me to the uttermost*
> *when I think about the Lord*
> *how he picked me up and turned me around*
> *how He set my feet on solid ground*
> *It makes me want to shout,*
> *"Hallelujah! Thank you, Jesus!*
> *Lord, you're worthy*
> *of all the glory, and all the honor and all the praise!"*[14]

When you reflect upon God's mercy, it moves you to worship. If a person does not want to worship God, it is simply because they do not know God, or are not focused on God. If you want to cultivate a heart of worship, begin

---

[14] Huey, James. "When I Think About the Lord," *Believe*. (Colorado Springs: Hosanna! Music, 1988).

by focusing on the goodness and the greatness of God. Read what the Bible has to say about Him. Listen to others testify about what He has done in their lives. Let yourself be overwhelmed by the beauty of creation. Think about how much God showed His love for you by sending Jesus to save and redeem you. The first step in worship is to view His mercies. The next step is come into His presence.

COME INTO HIS PRESENCE

God is a true living being. He invites you to draw into His presence. Worship is about coming into His presence. How else can you offer yourself or anything to Him? If all you think about in worship is attending a service or engaging in religious ritual, it will quickly lose its meaning and deteriorate into lifeless empty religion. Worship is about meeting with God. It is about coming into His presence. How do you draw into His presence? Psalm 100:4 says, *Enter into His gates with Thanks-giving, and into His courts with praise. Be thankful to Him, and bless His name* (NIV).

There are two attitudes essential to worship. There are two actions that will literally draw us into the presence of God. The first is thanksgiving and the second is praise. We looked at this verse in the chapter 3, but let us take a closer look at thanksgiving and praise here and just why they are so important.

Thanksgiving is the act of expressing gratitude to another. It begins with the recognition that you have received a gift or a blessing. It involves an expression of gratitude back to the giver. Thanksgiving is one of the most important attitudes in a person's life. 1 Thessalonians 5:18 says ...*give thanks in all circumstances; for this is the will of God in Christ Jesus for you* (ESV).

A grateful spirit is essential to a life of joy and health. You can be grumpy or you can be grateful, but you cannot be both at the same time. Every single person has reasons to be grumpy or grateful. You can focus on your losses or your wins, your burdens or your blessings. It is up to you. Thanksgiving is the deliberate step of focusing on your blessings, recognizing they come from God, and expressing your gratitude to Him.

Praise is focusing on the attributes of God and giving verbal affirmation of His attributes through words or deeds. Praise involves some kind of expression. When you praise another person, you speak good things about him or her. You tell them what you see and observe. You cannot praise another person and be silent. Praise demands an expression, usually verbal. When we praise God, we speak, or sing, or express in some fashion what we see in God and how we feel about God.

According to Psalm 100:4, thanksgiving opens the gate to God's presence and praise brings us into His courts. I like to think of it this way. Recently I was visiting a gated community in our area. For many reasons some of the nicer neighborhoods have gates that require a numerical code or special pass to get in. The person I was visiting had supplied me with the numerical code, and so when I drove up I pushed in the 4-digit code and the gate opened up. However, in this neighborhood I came to yet another gate that was blocking the very street on which the home was located. The owner had given me a second code to open the second gate. The first code got me into the subdivision, and the second code got me onto the street. Then I was able to drive right up to their house and meet with them. I envision worship that way. The first code gets me through the gates. The second gets me into the courts of God. When I get through both gates I am in His presence able to worship Him. The first code is thanksgiving. The second is praise.

When you are ready to approach God, start with a thankful spirit. That "code" opens up the gate and allows you to begin worship. Then continue with praise. Your affirmations of the greatness of God usher you into His presence. One gets you through the gates and the second gets you into His courts. Now you are ready to worship, and worship culminates in giving yourself to God.

GIVE YOURSELF TO GOD

We are motivated to worship by viewing God's mercy. We move to worship when we present ourselves to Him. Worship is more than bringing a song, or a financial gift, or sitting through a service. It is the presentation of the ultimate gift you can give, the gift of yourself. Imagine walking down to the front of the church and laying yourself on the altar, as if to say, "God, I belong to You, every single part of me is Yours." That is what worship is, bringing yourself to the Lord (Romans 12:1).

A sacrifice is a complete surrender. The humorous story is told of a chicken and the pig who both loved the farmer so much that they decided to fix him a big breakfast. The chicken suggested ham and eggs. The pig replied, "For you, that is an offering, but for me, that is a sacrifice!" God wants us to offer ourselves to Him as a living sacrifice, not a dead one. That is, He wants our very lives to be completely surrendered to Him. Again, in view of what He has done for us, it is the only reasonable response.

Look again at the defining verse on worship in Deuteronomy 6:5 *Love the LORD your God with all your heart and with all your soul and with all your strength.*

In Mark 12:30, Jesus quoted this verse and added the word *mind* to the list. Most likely, the word *mind* simply expounds on what it means to love God with all our physical strength. What the verse is saying is that you are to love God with your entire being. You are to give everything you are to God and love Him with every part of your life.

What are some of the ways you express your love to God? You can love God *emotionally.* When the Bible says to love Him with all your heart, surely it speaks of your emotions, your feelings. We are emotional beings. We feel. We can feel happiness and excitement, enthusiasm or sadness. The range of emotions is complex and it is part of how God made you. While emotions are not supposed to control your life or direct your decisions, life would be quite boring if you did not have emotions. Can you imagine a love relationship with someone where you did not express your feelings? That would be very dull.

How do you express your feelings to God? You can certainly talk to God and tell Him how you feel, but when people really want to express their deepest emotions, they use ways that transcend mere words. That is where art comes in. Art is the way people express what they feel. Now, there are many ways to express yourself such as dancing, sculpting, painting, and yes, music. Music moves us. The right kind of music can touch your heart in places nobody else can go. The right song, the right sounds, can bring tears to your eyes, a smile to your face, or cause you to dance (or want to dance) with joy. It is the power of a song. Maybe that is why music is so prominent in the Bible and why music has such an important role in our worship. Look at what the Bible says about worship and music.

- *Shout for joy to the LORD, all the earth, burst into jubilant song with music; make music to the LORD with the harp, with the harp and the sound of singing.* Psalm 98:4-5 NIV

- *About midnight Paul and Silas were praying and singing hymns to God, and the other prisoners were listening to them.* Acts 16:25 NIV

- *Then I heard every creature in heaven and on earth and under the earth and on the sea, and all that is in them, singing: "To him who sits on the throne and to the Lamb be praise and honor and glory and power, forever and ever!"* Revelation 5:13 NIV

- *I will sing to the LORD, for he has been good to me.* Psalm 13:6 NIV

- *Sing joyfully to the LORD, you righteous; it is fitting for the upright to praise him. Praise the LORD with the harp; make music to him on the ten-stringed lyre. Sing to him a new song; play skillfully, and shout for joy.* Psalm 33:1-3 NIV

- *Sing to the LORD with thanksgiving; make music to our God on the harp.* Psalm 147:7 NIV

- *Speak to one another with psalms, hymns and spiritual songs. Sing and make music in your heart to the Lord.* Ephesians 5:19 NIV

In fact, music is so critical to worship that there is an entire book in the Bible devoted to the songs of worship, the book of Psalms. Did you know that there are 77 commands in the Psalms to sing? Music opens our heart and allows us to express our deep feelings to God.

That is why music should play such an important part of your worship experience. Participate in the worship at church. Sing the songs from your heart and offer your praise to the Lord. Use Christian music in your car and in your home to lift your spirit and direct your attention to

God. Sing to the Lord.

Worship should be emotional. In the Psalms, there are commands to lift your hands (134:2), dance (149:3), shout (100:1), clap your hands (47:1), and sometimes just to be quiet (46:10). Since you have a wide range of emotions, there is a wide range of ways to express those emotions. Remember that different people express their emotions differently. They do not all have to respond like you. Find your way to express your emotions to God.

We should also worship God *intellectually.* Jesus said we should love God with our entire mind. How do you love God with your mind? By focusing your thoughts upon God. You pay attention to things you love. Let a sports fan see his favorite team on television and suddenly his focus is riveted. The Bible says to *Set your mind on things above* (Colossians 3:2 NKJV).

You can do this by disciplining yourself to spend time alone with God every day. Spend some time reading His Word and talking to Him every day. Make sure you attend worship, and not out of obligation but out of a desire to focus on God. Ask God to keep your mind and thoughts focused during worship. Take notes. Pay attention. Focus on God. Worship Him with your mind.

We should also worship God *financially.* Giving is a huge part of worship. In the Bible, people gave as they valued the things of God and wanted to express their thanksgiving. In 2 Samuel 24, David needed to buy a piece of ground to offer a sacrifice to the Lord. The ground was owned by a man named Araunah, and because he was a willing servant of David, he offered to give the land to David. The Bible says,

But the king replied to Araunah, "No, I insist on paying you for it. I will not sacrifice to the LORD my God burnt offerings that cost me nothing." 2 Samuel 24:24 NIV

David understood that giving was an expression of worship and he was unwilling to offer a sacrifice that did not cost him something. Some people in the Bible were just going through the motions of worship. They brought gifts that were cheap, damaged, or flawed. God saw through their hypocrisy and rebuked them. In Malachi 1, God spoke through His prophet and said,

> *"When you bring blind animals for sacrifice, is that not wrong? When you sacrifice crippled or diseased animals, is that not wrong? Try offering them to your governor! Would he be pleased with you? Would he accept you?" says the LORD Almighty.* Malachi 1:8 NIV

God does not want or need your money. He wants something much more valuable. He wants you, all of you. When you give yourself to the Lord, then it is easy to give your money as well. Our giving is one way we bring ourselves to Him and worship Him.

We should also worship God *physically*. Jesus said to love God with all our strength. How do you love God with your strength? Use your work and your abilities for God. When you work, work for Him. All labor, whether it is manual labor, menial labor, secular labor, or ministry is supposed to be an act of worship. Colossians 3:23-24 says,

> *Whatever you do, work at it with all your heart, as working for the Lord, not for men, since you know that you will receive an inheritance from the Lord as a reward. It is the Lord Christ you are serving.* (NIV)

Do not compartmentalize your life. Do not say, "I work here for money, and there for the Lord!" No. Everything you do is for the Lord. Now, imagine how that attitude will transform your job. When you get up tomorrow morning and go to work, do not work for a paycheck — you are worth more than that! — work for God. Turn your work into worship. Do not just work for a person, work for the Lord. Picture God watching all that you do, and determine to give your best to Him because He gave His best for you.

Love God with your heart, your soul, your mind, and your strength. Worship Him emotionally, intellectually, financially, and physically. When you give your all to Him, that is worship; it is a living sacrifice. We do this because He has given so much to us. We love Him because He first loved us, and when we love Him and give ourselves completely to Him, well, that is what worship is all about!

Growth Steps

Take these growth steps to discover dynamic life:

- Attend public worship with other believers every week. The habit and practice of worshipping God with others should be a lifelong habit.
- Listen to Christian music. Find the style that speaks to you. Buy some new music this week. There are all kinds of Christian music. When you are in the car, at home, or working out, listen to music that touches your heart and magnifies the Lord. Sing along. Let God hear your voice and receive your praises.
- Write out your top 10 reasons to be thankful, and the top 10 attributes of God. Focus on your lists. Be thankful and give God praise.
- When you do attend worship, prepare your heart; do not just go through the religious motions. Come before Him with singing. Enter His gates with thanksgiving and His courts with praise.

Devotional Guide

Read through these passages over the next week and write your observations, questions, and applications to your life.

Monday:	Luke 19:37-40
Tuesday:	Acts 16:22-31
Wednesday:	Ephesians 5:17-21
Thursday:	2 Chronicles 20:14-22
Friday:	Revelation 5:8-14
Weekend:	Psalm 96; Luke 24:45-53

This Week's Memory Verse

You are worthy, our Lord and God, to receive glory and honor and power, for you created all things, and by your will they were created and have their being. Revelation 4:11 NIV

Chapter Seven

Invest in God's Kingdom
The Discipline of Giving

...but lay up for yourselves treasures in heaven, where neither moth nor rust destroys and where thieves do not break in and steal.
Matthew 6:20 (NKJV)

TREASURE IN HEAVEN

Everyone loves a great investment. Who does not want to turn a little into a lot? Would you believe that Jesus has some great investment advice? Jesus said, *"Lay your treasure up in heaven."* You cannot take it with you, but according to Jesus, you can send it on ahead. Investing in God's kingdom makes sense. It will last and it brings a great return. Learning to view life from an eternal perspective and learning to use your resources to invest in that which lasts forever is a major step toward dynamic life. This is the sixth discipline necessary to grow spiritually. You need to learn to be generous. You need to develop an eternal perspective with your material resources. You need to invest in God's kingdom. When you do, it not only brings a financial dividend in eternity, it also has a spiritual impact here and now. A generous life builds you up on the inside, makes you more like Jesus, and helps you discover dynamic life.

In 1 Timothy 6:17-19, Paul gave believers important counsel:

> *Command those who are rich in this present world not to be arrogant nor to put their hope in wealth, which is so uncertain, but to put their hope in God, who richly provides us with everything for our enjoyment. Command them to do good, to be rich in good deeds, and to be generous and willing to share. In this way they will lay up treasure for themselves as a firm foundation for the coming age, so that they may take hold of the life that is truly life.* (NIV)

In this chapter, we will look at three key steps you must take to develop the proper perspective on money and eternity.

GIVE GOD CONTROL

People who refuse to give are not just greedy, they are deceived. They have not seen the truth about themselves, about life, and mostly about God. If they could just see the truth from an eternal perspective, they would realize that giving is the greatest investment they could ever make. A failure to give is a failure to trust God.

In verse 17, Paul implored us to put our hope in God, not in personal wealth. When it comes to money, some people find it really hard to trust God. This is because we think money can give us happiness and security. We think, "If I just had a little more, if I could just buy 'it,' then I would be happy." Someone asked a wealthy man once how much was enough. His reply was "just a little more."

It is that deception that causes so much financial bondage. Many of us think that if we could just have enough stuff, then we would truly be happy. So we end up buying things we can't afford, we live beyond our means, and we rake up a disabling debt. The cycle just gets worse and worse until some people find themselves so underwater financially that they don't even know how to get out. Even if we are wise at money management and avoid some of the common pitfalls, we still can end up disappointed and disillusioned. Money really doesn't buy happiness. It can make life easier in some ways, but it can also make it harder in others. All you have to do is look around to realize that money does not guarantee happiness.

Money also does not guarantee security. The Bible warns us about the foolishness of believing that some amount of financial wealth can make us secure (Proverbs 23:5).

After the Great Depression, stories were told and retold of men who took their lives because they had lost their fortunes. In reality, no amount of money can guarantee real security. As Jesus taught, money is temporary and uncertain. It can be gone in a moment.

Even if your money seems secure and safe, it still cannot prevent death. You may be able to buy the finest medical care, but nothing can prevent the fact that one day your earthly life will end. At its very best and most secure, money is still temporary.

John Ortberg in his book *When the Game is Over, It All Goes Back in the Box* compared the treasures of this life to the play money used in the game Monopoly™. He spoke of growing up and playing his grandmother in the familiar game. He finally got good enough to win the game. He was elated. He looked at all his houses and hotels. He relished the ownership of all the strategic properties and the defeat of his competitors. Then he had a sad realization, which hit for the first time, since this time he had emerged victorious. After the game, it all goes back in the box. All the houses, all the hotels; it all goes back in the box. Someone else will own them another day, and someone else will play the game. Everything he "owned" was in reality just a game, just temporary.[15] Your possessions may seem more real than Monopoly money, but honestly, that is just a matter of time and perspective. Everything you won will also go back in the box one day. No matter how secure you think it is, it is really just temporary.

That is why the Bible instructs us to put our hope in God. God is not temporary; He is secure. He is trustworthy. People who put their hope in God realize that it all comes from Him anyway. When you trust God then you can obey whatever God tells you to do. Trusting God does not take the work out of life, but it does take the worry out of life. You need to take the important step of giving God control of

---

[15] Ortberg, John, *When the Game is Over, It All Goes Back in the Box*. (Grand Rapids: Zondervan, 2007).

your material possessions. When you give God control, it means understanding three important principles.

OWNERSHIP

The first is the principle of *ownership*. God owns it all. When you trust God, you know where it all comes from. God has given you everything you have. You may not believe that. You might object and say, "I am a self-made person." You might say, "I've worked hard and earned what I have received." Who gave you the ability to work hard? Who gave you the abilities that have allowed you to prosper? Did you have anything to do with where you were born, or what gifts or talents you received? Yes, you may have worked hard, but God is still the owner of it all. When you die, it will belong to someone else. It will not be yours. Truthfully, it all belongs to God. He can give and He can take away. God says, *For every beast of the forest is Mine, and the cattle on a thousand hills* (Psalm 50:10 NKJV).

God is the owner. He can take care of your needs, and He has promised to do that if you trust in Him. God is the greatest giver of all. Paul said, *God…richly provides us with everything for our enjoyment* (1 Timothy 6:18 NIV).

God can more than adequately take care of your needs. When you trust Him and begin to put God's will and God's purpose first, He has promised to provide for your needs.

Jesus invites us to invest first in the kingdom of God and then trust Him for everything else. Most people do exactly the opposite. We worry about what we need first, and then invest in God's kingdom if we have anything left over. We get it backward. Jesus said, *Seek the Kingdom of God above all else, and live righteously, and he will give you everything you need* (Matthew 6:33 NLT). And in Philippians 4:19, Paul wrote, *And my God shall supply all your need according to*

His riches in glory by Christ Jesus (NKJV).

You can trust God. He owns it anyway. You can opt to live your life believing you are in control, but you are deceiving yourself. The other option is to confess the truth, that God owns it all, and give Him control. The first step to financial freedom is recognizing the truth about ownership. Give it all to God. You might even want to make up a quick claim deed just between you and God. Sign everything you have over to God. Confess that He owns it all — the money, the land, the houses, the accounts, everything. He owns it, and you are His servant. When you recognize the truth about ownership, you are ready for the second principle.

LORDSHIP

The second principle you must understand is *lordship*. The principle of lordship means that you understand that God is the boss, and therefore He is in charge. You agree to follow His wisdom and commands. You can only do this if you really trust Him, but if you do, you will find that it is worth it. You see, the Bible is full of financial wisdom. If you will apply God's wisdom into your financial life, you will save yourself from financial bondage (or get out of bondage, and yes it is possible) and free yourself up to live generously. Most churches have financial courses that will help you learn biblical principles in regard to finance. I encourage you to take one of those courses and begin to learn how to live in financial freedom.

One of the basic things you will learn from God's Word is the importance of planning. Sometimes we call this a budget. You have to tell your money where to go or it will end up telling you where to go. You have to establish the right priorities and learn to live within your means. An essential to financial freedom is learning to live on less than you make.

Another important truth in God's Word is learning the dangers of debt. Using tomorrow's money to get what we want today is a surefire way into financial bondage. The Bible warns about the danger of debt (Proverbs 22:7).

The Bible is filled with many other practical financial insights such as the importance of saving. The point I am making is that when you agree to give God control, then you agree to follow His commands, and His commands will lead you to financial peace, stability, and possibly even prosperity. One of the main reasons many people do not give more is because they are in such financial bondage that they really cannot afford to give. If you want to invest in God's kingdom, you will need to get your financial house in order so that you can do it.

STEWARDSHIP

Then there is the principle of *stewardship.* Essentially your role is that of a money manager. The money you have really isn't yours, it is God's. Your role is to manage that in a way that pleases Him. He does want to bless you. As Paul wrote He *richly provides us with everything for our enjoyment* (1 Timothy 6:18 NIV).

But God also cares about His kingdom, He cares about people who need to hear the gospel, He cares about needs around the world, and He cares about the poor. God wants you to steward the resources that He has entrusted to you, and Jesus taught that He will one day hold you accountable for what you did with those resources.

Jesus communicated the truths about ownership, lordship, and stewardship in a story He told.

Again, the Kingdom of Heaven can be illustrated by the story of a man going on a long trip. He called together his servants and entrusted his money to them while he was gone. He gave

*five bags of silver to one, two bags of silver to another, and one
bag of silver to the last – dividing it in proportion to their
abilities. He then left on his trip. The servant who received the
five bags of silver began to invest the money and earned five
more. The servant with two bags of silver also went to work
and earned two more. But the servant who received the one bag
of silver dug a hole in the ground and hid the master's money.
After a long time their master returned from his trip and called
them to give an account of how they had used his money.*
Matthew 25:14-19 NLT

God is the owner. He entrusts His resources to you,
the steward, and He will one day return to ask you what
you did with what He gave you. That is why you should
give God control now. Recognize Him as the owner of it all.
Follow His commands and guidelines and use the resources
under your care to invest in God's kingdom. After you give
God control, you are ready to take the next step.

DEVELOP A GENEROUS SPIRIT

Look again at 1 Timothy 6:18: *Command them to do
good, to be rich in good deeds, and to be generous and willing to
share* (NIV).
God wants you to learn to be a giver. He wants you
to be generous in investing in things besides yourself. He
especially wants you to invest in His kingdom. Giving is a
vital part of being a follower of Christ. The verb *give* is
found in the Bible more than the verbs believe, pray, and
love put together. Look at these verses on giving,

- *It is more blessed to give than to receive.* Acts 20:35 NIV

- *Give, and it will be given to you.* Luke 6:38 NIV

- *A generous man will prosper; he who refreshes others will himself be refreshed.* Proverbs 11:25 NIV

- *God loves a cheerful giver.* 2 Corinthians 9:7 NIV

- *…see that you also excel in this grace of giving.* 2 Corinthians 8:7 NIV

In life, there are givers and takers. God wants you to be a giver. It is an essential part of dynamic life. Let's look at several key questions related to giving.

WHY GIVE?

First, giving builds your character. You are never more like God than when you give. As John 3:16 says, *God so loved the world He gave …* (NIV).

If you want to grow in Christ-like character, you will have to learn to be generous. Giving is one of the things that God uses to mold your character and help you grow.

Second, giving brings joy. There is something about giving that causes people to be filled with joy and happiness. Think about it. How many stingy, greedy people do you know who are truly happy? I mean happy like they are ready to double over laughing happy. The happiest people I know love to give. I challenge you to look around, and I think you will find the same thing is true in your life. The people who have the most peace, the most joy, and the healthiest perspective on life are people who love to give to others.

Third, there is a practical reason to give. God's work relies on the support of God's people. If the church is to expand, and if the gospel is to go forth into the ends of the earth, then God's people will have to supply the resources. God uses you to help get His work done. In the Bible, we read of three women who financially supported Jesus' ministry.

> *After this, Jesus traveled about from one town and village to another, proclaiming the good news of the kingdom of God....Mary...Joanna...Susanna... These women were helping to support them out of their own means.* Luke 8:1-3 NIV

Paul thanked the Philippian church for their faithful support of his ministry (Philippians 4:15-16).

There is also a financial reason to give. While some teachers have misused this important principle, it is clear that God promises a financial blessing to those who are faithful to give. This is not a way of manipulating God or using a spiritual step to gain financial wealth. God promises that when we place Him first and give generously and according to His principles that He will bless us financially, provide for our needs, and allow us to give even more.

> *Remember this: Whoever sows sparingly will also reap sparingly, and whoever sows generously will also reap generously...Now he who supplies seed to the sower and bread for food will also supply and increase your store of seed and will enlarge the harvest of your righteousness. You will be made rich in every way so that you can be generous on every occasion, and through us your generosity will result in thanksgiving to God.* 2 Corinthians 9:6-7,10-11 NIV

HOW DO YOU GIVE?

You need to give generously and with the proper motive.

What does generous giving look like? How much does God expect you to give? Ultimately, you and God will have to decide that.

Each man should give what he has decided in his heart to give, not reluctantly or under compulsion, for God loves a cheerful giver. 2 Corinthians 9:7 NIV

I know that you should give generously, motivated by His grace for you.

For I testify that they gave as much as they were able, and even beyond their ability. Entirely on their own . . . For you know the grace of our Lord Jesus Christ, that though he was rich, yet for your sakes he became poor, so that you through his poverty might become rich. 2 Corinthians 8:3,9 NIV

There is a biblical standard of giving taught in the Old Testament. It is tithing. The tithe is a tenth, 10% of a given amount. In the Old Testament, God's people were taught that a tithe of their income belonged to God. They learned to give 10% of everything they took in. The Bible says,

A tithe of everything from the land, whether grain from the soil or fruit from the trees, belongs to the Lord; it is holy to the Lord. Leviticus 27:30 NIV

Tithing is found throughout the Old Testament. There were various types of tithing for various purposes but the principle was always the same: 10% belonged to God. When God's people failed to tithe, God accused them of robbing Him. The Old Testament prophet Malachi brought harsh words for those who refused to tithe,

"Will a man rob God? Yet you have robbed Me! But you say, 'In what way have we robbed You?' In tithes and offerings." Malachi 3:8 NKJV

Jesus mentioned tithing in the New Testament. He was addressing the religious leaders of His day who were tithing but missing the bigger issue of godly character. This shows that people can tithe out of religious duty and still have a heart that is hard toward the things of God. You can give without loving, but you cannot love without giving. Jesus did not criticize their practice of tithing, and He did not overturn it. Actually, He commended them for tithing at the same time He criticized them for missing the big picture.

What sorrow awaits you teachers of religious law and you Pharisees. Hypocrites! For you are careful to tithe even the tiniest income from your herb gardens, but you ignore the more important aspects of the law – justice, mercy, and faith. You should tithe, yes, but do not neglect the more important things. Matthew 23:23 NLT

If Jesus did not want us to tithe, He could have said so at that point. Instead, He commended the Pharisees for tithing even though they missed the bigger point. Some Christians argue today that tithing is no longer an obligation for Christians. However, nowhere in the New Testament does it say that we should not pay attention to this Old Testament standard of giving. Furthermore, if we gave generously it would probably be a moot point. The average Christian in America gives less than 2% of their income away. It is hard to believe that such a meager amount represents generous giving when there is a clear biblical standard to give more.

Tithing is a brilliant way to learn generous giving. We all need disciplines and standards in our life. Tithing teaches proportional giving. If you make ten dollars, give one; if you make one hundred, give ten; if you make one thousand, give one hundred; and so on. The percentage is the same for everyone. It is clear and easy to understand, and to whom much is given, much is required. It also teaches consistent giving. Every time God blesses me with income, every paycheck, I give a portion of it back to Him.

I am very grateful that I learned to tithe at a young age. I learned to tithe when I was still a child, and when I gradually began to earn a few dollars as a teenager it was a natural simple step to give 10% away. In early adulthood, I didn't make much money, but the tithe always came first. As I grew older my tithe increased, and eventually so did the actual percentage I gave away. I am glad I learned to tithe early on. It became a habit in my life and my giving has gradually increased with my income. If it had not been for the standard of the tithe, I am fairly certain that I would not have learned generous giving as quickly as I did.

Tithing is a great standard for you to embrace as you begin your journey toward generous giving. If you are just starting out, it can be a fairly easy habit to build into your life, the sooner the better. Start young and it will simply become a financial habit. If you come to Christ later on in your life, or realize later in adulthood that you need to begin tithing, it can be a harder adjustment. You may have to arrange your budget differently. You may need to downsize some things in order to free up a tithe in your budget. It is worth it. Whatever you have to do is worth it. If tithing seems impossible, let me encourage you to take these simple steps. First, get your financial house in order. Get on a budget and begin to reduce debt. Second, start giving. Start with whatever amount you can, but begin to practice regular consistent giving. Third, take the steps necessary to move toward being able to give a tenth away. It may take a little time and you may have to make some painful adjustment, but I encourage you to move quickly in that direction. I have never met a person who regularly tithed who regretted it.

And by the way, God promises to bless those who tithe. God said through His prophet Malachi,

> *"Bring the whole tithe into the storehouse, that there may be food in my house. Test me in this," says the Lord Almighty, "and see if I will not throw open the floodgates of heaven and pour out so much blessing that you will not have room enough for it."* Malachi 3:10 NIV

There are other types of giving in the Bible besides tithing. Tithing formed the foundation of a generous lifestyle, but God's people were also eager to give above and beyond the tithe to special opportunities that came up. Sometimes these were called "free will" offerings. Sometimes these offerings were taken to support a building project, and sometimes they were taken to have a celebration.

> *They received from Moses all the offerings the Israelites had brought to carry out the work of constructing the sanctuary. And the people continued to bring freewill offerings morning after morning.* Exodus 36:3 NIV

There will be many opportunities for you to practice generosity. There are also many commands to give to the poor.

- *For there will never cease to be poor in the land. Therefore I command you, 'You shall open wide your hand to your brother, to the needy and to the poor, in your land.* Deuteronomy 15:11 ESV

- *Whoever is generous to the poor lends to the Lord, and he will repay him for his deed.* Proverbs 19:17 ESV

- *A generous man will himself be blessed for he shares his food with the poor.* Proverbs 22:9 NIV

When you give, it is not just the amount that matters, but also the motive. As with all religious disciplines, it is possible to forget the purpose. In Jesus' times there were religious leaders who practiced some good spiritual disciplines, but for absolutely the wrong reasons. They prayed, gave, and even fasted so that other people would be impressed. Your goal in giving should never be to impress others; it should be to honor God. Jesus said,

> So when you give to the needy, do not announce it with trumpets, as the hypocrites do in the synagogues and on the streets, to be honored by men. I tell you the truth, they have received their reward in full. But when you give to the needy, do not let your left hand know what your right hand is doing, so that your giving may be in secret. Then your Father, who sees what is done in secret, will reward you. Matthew 6:2-4 NIV

If you are going to excel in the practice of giving, it is going to take discipline and setting priorities. In every budget something must come first. When the Bible talks about giving, it teaches us to give our first and our best to God. If you wait and give God the leftovers, there may not be much left. Instead, you should give to God the first part (Proverbs 3:9). The first fruit was the very first part of the harvest, that which came first. Your giving should be the first part of your budget, off the top, not out of the bottom.

We have talked about why you should give and how you should give, now I want to deal with one final question,

WHERE DO YOU GIVE?

There are no shortage of opportunities to give. Charitable organizations, fundraisers, educational institutions, and religious ministries abound, and sometimes it feels like everyone is asking you to give. First, you need to remember that you are giving to the Lord. You do not give because you feel pressured or obligated; in fact, that is the wrong reason to give. You should give because you want to. You should give first to the Lord.

In the Bible, there is a clear pattern of giving at the place where you worship God. For us that is the local church. In the Old Testament, they brought their offerings to the temple (Nehemiah 10:38; Exodus 34:26)

In the New Testament, they brought their gift to church leaders to be distributed accordingly.

> *For from time to time those who owned lands or houses sold them, brought the money from the sales and put it at the apostles' feet, and it was distributed to anyone as he had need.* Acts 4:34-35 NIV

> *What is more, he was chosen by the churches to accompany us as we carry the offering, which we administer in order to honor the Lord himself and to show our eagerness to help. We want to avoid any criticism of the way we administer this liberal gift. For we are taking pains to do what is right, not only in the eyes of the Lord but also in the eyes of men.* 2 Corinthians 8:19-21 NIV

I believe it is the pattern of scripture and that it makes the most sense to give your tithe through your local church. The local church touches every area of ministry. When people give through the church they support pre-school ministry, children's ministry, student ministry, family ministry, senior adult ministry, visitation, ministry to the sick, ministry to the poor, counseling, worship ministry, missions, not to mention the teaching and preaching of the gospel. Every conceivable ministry is supported through the local church. And because it is your local church, you are closer to the decision-making process. You can ask questions, get information, and have a greater degree of comfort that your offerings are being used to support God's work. You see it in action.

When you are sick, or there is a need in your family, chances are it will be your local church that will be there to help and minister to you. So I encourage you to tithe through your local church.

There are also many other worthy ministries you can support. You can give above and beyond your tithe to these opportunities. There are charitable organizations that do good work and create opportunities to give to the poor and needy. You should be wise and thoughtful about where you give. Do your homework. Ask the right questions. Make sure your giving is making the impact you want it to make. Remember, you are a steward, and a steward needs to manage resources wisely.

WHAT REALLY MATTERS

As you learn to live generously, you will grow in your faith and move toward the dynamic life that God has for you. You will be doing one of the most important things you can do to be happy, healthy, and holy. You will be pleasing God. You will show wisdom by investing in God's kingdom. And it will pay eternal dividends.

In the famous movie *Schindler's List*, the true story is told of German businessman Oscar Schindler. Schindler found a way to employ Jewish laborers during World War II deep inside Poland. He established a factory that would hire Jews who otherwise would have been shipped to concentration camps. He could do this inexpensively since he did not have to pay them a fair wage and therefore he could turn huge profits. What began as a money making venture turned into a humanitarian one as he realized what was happening to the Jewish people, and when he realized that the Jews he employed would not be taken off to the camps and near certain death. He began to hire more and more people, even more than he needed to do the work. It is estimated that he saved more than 1,200 people from death due to his actions.

At the end of the war, the Jews were liberated and as Schindler prepared to leave, he met with some of those he saved one final time. They expressed their deep gratitude. However, Schindler broke down and began to weep. Instead of relishing their gratitude, he was haunted by the regret that he did not do more. In the movie, he looks at his pen and says, "I can't believe I kept this pen. I could have sold it and saved two more." Then he looks at his expensive car and says, "I kept this car! I could have sold this car and bought ten more." With deep regret, he finally says, "If I just hadn't wasted so much."

One day in eternity, we will see what really mattered. I wonder if we will be amazed that we spent so much time on things that mattered so little. Make sure you live in such a way that in eternity you will rejoice that you invested in people and that you helped expand God's kingdom. Lay your treasure up where it lasts forever.

16 Schindler's List. Prod./Dir. Steven Spielberg. Perf. **Liam** Neeson, Ralf Fiennes, Ben Kingsley. DVD. Universal Pictures & Amblin Entertainment, 1993

Growth Steps

Take these growth steps to discover dynamic life:

- Write your own quit claim deed (see Resources section) and sign everything over to God. Acknowledge that everything you own is really His, and that you not only understand that principle, but you desire to be a faithful steward of His resources.
- Get your financial house in order. Make you sure you have a clear understanding of how much is coming in and how much is going out. Develop a budget and begin to live within your means.
- Reduce debt. If you have indebtedness, begin to work on a plan to aggressively reduce and eliminate debt. This may take a while but it can usually happen quicker than you think. Begin to move in the right direction.
- If you need some financial guidance, enroll in a class at your church that teaches biblical financial principles.
- Start giving. Make this a permanent practice in your life, for the rest of your life.
- Identify what giving away a tithe would look like in your life. What is your tithe? Identify the steps you need to take to be able to give away at least a tenth of your income.

Devotional Guide

Read through these passages over the next week and write your observations, questions, and applications to your life.

Monday:	Mark 12:41-44
Tuesday:	2 Corinthians 9:6-15
Wednesday:	Mark 10:23-31
Thursday:	Exodus 35:20-29; 36:2-5
Friday:	Acts 5:1-11

Weekend: Luke 18:18-23; Psalm 37

This Week's Memory Verse

... but lay up for yourselves treasures in heaven, where neither moth nor rust destroys and where thieves do not break in and steal. Matthew 6:20 NIV

Chapter Eight

Contagiously Influence Others
The Discipline of Sharing Your Faith

Be wise in the way you act toward outsiders; make the most of
every opportunity. Let your conversation be always full of grace,
seasoned with salt, so that you may know how to answer everyone.
Colossians 4:5-6 (NIV)

WITNESSES

God wants to use you. God's plan is consistent throughout the Bible. He blesses someone to be a blessing. When He first called Abram and promised to bless Him, it was for the ultimate purpose of using Him to bless the nations of the world.

> *I will make you into a great nation and I will bless you; I will make your name great, and you will be a blessing.* Genesis 12:2 NIV

God reiterated His promise to Abraham's great-grandson Jacob, reminding him that God was blessing Jacob so that through him, the world would be blessed (Genesis 28:14). On numerous occasions, God reminded His people Israel that they were blessed to be a blessing (Psalm 67:7).

Even Jonah learned that God cared about the people of Nineveh (modern day Iraq) more than Jonah's own comfort and convenience. It was a hard lesson for him to learn, and it is a hard lesson for us to remember. God cares about people.

In the New Testament, Jesus came to remind the religious establishment that God cared more about people than He did their empty religious traditions and puffed up self-righteousness. Jesus clearly stated His mission on earth when He said, *For the Son of Man came to seek and to save what was lost* (Luke 19:10 NIV). He gave the mission to His church when He said,

- *But you will receive power when the Holy Spirit comes on you; and you will be my witnesses in Jerusalem, and in all Judea and Samaria, and to the ends of the earth.* Acts 1:8 NIV

- *Therefore go and make disciples of all nations, baptizing them in the name of the Father and of the Son and of the Holy Spirit, and teaching them to obey everything I have commanded you. And surely I am with you always, to the very end of the age.* Matthew 28:19-20 NIV

- *…repentance and forgiveness of sins will be preached in his name to all nations, beginning at Jerusalem. You are witnesses of these things.* Luke 24:47-49 NIV

Again and again, the mission is repeated in a clear, unmistakable call to be witnesses for Jesus. Paul reminded the early believers of God's call on their life when he said,

And all of this is a gift from God, who brought us back to himself through Christ. And God has given us this task of reconciling people to him. 2 Corinthians 5:18 NLT

Three facts are clear. First, God has the power to change lives. Second, God wants to save people. Third, God wants to use you to do it. He has given you the job, the ministry, of reconciliation. God works through people to bring people into His family. He uses ordinary people just like you.

So how are you doing? Are you fulfilling God's plan by influencing others for God? Are there people hearing the message and checking out what it means to be a Christ-follower because of the influence you have in their lives?

This is the final discipline we need to cover in discover dynamic life. You need to contagiously influence others.

The temptation and tendency that Christians have is to get so comfortable in the church that we forget about the world around us. If you aren't careful, you can find yourself living in a Christian bubble, hanging out with Christians, going to church, even a Christian school or Christian entertainment. All of that is good and has its place, but when and where are you going to fulfill God's plan by influencing others around you? Remember, God cares about people who are spiritually lost. The more that religious people grow unconcerned about those who are still far off from God, the more corrupt and lukewarm their faith will become until it is a faint echo of what God intended.

Everything God has done and is doing in your life is for a reason, a purpose. It isn't just about you receiving God's blessing. God wants to use you, work through you, and just as He did for Abraham, He wants to bless you to bless others.

One of the myths that some church people have is that there are only a select few who can successfully influence outsiders. We think that since there are a few really bold people, intellectually gifted in understanding and explaining the faith, and eager to tackle the world, that we can just let those people do it. Or we think it is the professional's job. Pastors, evangelists, and TV superstars — they are the ones who can reach the world. But that isn't God's plan. The truth is that there are people you can influence who will never be influenced by a pastor or a TV personality, and who in all probability aren't going to just wake up next week and decide to check out a church. If someone is going to influence them, that someone is going to have to be you.

Now, here's the good news. You don't have to be someone else to do what God can use you to do. You don't have to be a preacher, or a superstar, or someone with different gifts and a different personality. God made you to be you because He wanted you. You are the one God can use. You are the one who can make the difference. You are the one who can influence others if you will just let God work through you.

If you want to influence someone's life, you might as well learn from the very best: Jesus. In John 4, you find the story of the Samaritan woman. We looked at it in chapter 1 to see how Jesus offered the woman real life, living water. Now, look at it from a different angle. Observe how Jesus engaged her in a spiritual conversation.

Jesus and His disciples were making their way through Samaria and about lunchtime Jesus engaged a Samaritan woman in conversation. By the time the day was over, the entire town was buzzing with excitement over the spiritual truth that had been revealed. This happened because Jesus followed three simple steps. These three steps can lead you to be a powerful influence for the gospel.

STEP ONE: INITIATE RELATIONSHIPS

Now he had to go through Samaria. So he came to a town in Samaria called Sychar, near the plot of ground Jacob had given to his son Joseph. Jacob's well was there, and Jesus, tired as he was from the journey, sat down by the well. It was about the sixth hour. When a Samaritan woman came to draw water, Jesus said to her, "Will you give me a drink?" (His disciples had gone into the town to buy food.) The Samaritan woman said to him, "You are a Jew and I am a Samaritan woman. How can you ask me for a drink?" (For Jews do not associate with Samaritans.) Jesus answered her, "If you knew the gift of God and who it is that asks you for a drink, you would have asked him and he would have given you living water." "Sir," the woman said, "you have nothing to draw with and the well is deep. Where can you get this living water? Are you greater than our father Jacob, who gave us the well and drank from it himself, as did also his sons and his flocks and herds?" Jesus answered, "Everyone who drinks this water will be thirsty again, but whoever drinks the water I give him will never thirst. Indeed, the water I give him will become in him a spring of water welling up to eternal life." The woman said to him,

"Sir, give me this water so that I won't get thirsty and have to keep coming here to draw water." John 4:4-15 NIV

In order to influence someone you have to have some kind of relationship. In His most famous sermon Jesus called on us to be salt and light. He called His followers the *salt of the earth* and the *light of the world*. What do salt and light have in common? They are agents of change. But salt doesn't do any good when it stays in a saltshaker, and a light doesn't help anyone if it is hidden under a bowl. Influence begins when you open up and get to know somebody.

In this story, Jesus found a way to strike up a quick conversation and even a quick friendship. That conversation opened up the opportunity to talk about spiritual things and uncover the incredible need in this woman's life.

The first part of initiating relationships is that you have to meet people on their own turf; you have to go to where they are. Verse 4 indicates that He needed to go through Samaria. Now we don't know if that means He had to go through Samaria for a practical reason, or for a spiritual reason. Normally, strict Jews avoided Samaria because of racial, religious, and cultural prejudice. Jews didn't like Samaritans. Racism is nothing new. Jews avoided Samaritans then like you might avoid a mangy dog. While Samaria may have been the most direct route from Judea to Galilee, it certainly wasn't the favored route.

The relationship would never have happened if Jesus hadn't gone through Samaria. When you think about it, isn't that what Jesus always did? Isn't that what Jesus did when He left heaven and came to earth? Didn't He come to our Samaria, and if He hadn't taken the initiative, do you think any of us could have ever found Him? In fact, the Bible makes it clear that God took the initiative to reach us (1 John 4:19).

In his book *Just Walk Across the Room*, Bill Hybels claims that our work of influencing others begins with just taking a walk across a room, or an office, or a ball field. It is taking the first step to go and meet someone: "Hi, my name is____. What's yours?" Just getting to know someone, and what is going on in their life, can suddenly open the door to spiritual influence. In the introduction to Hybel's book, he writes,

> *What if you knew that by simply crossing the room and saying hello to someone, you could change that person's life forever? Just a few steps to make an eternal difference. It has nothing to do with methods and everything to do with taking a genuine interest in another human being. All you need is a heart that's in tune with the Holy Spirit and a willingness to venture out of your 'Circle of Comfort' and into another person's life.*[16]

The first part of initiating relationships is that you have to take the first step. You have to go where they are. You have to walk across the street and find out who your neighbor is. Take the time after practice to get to know your child's coach. Go to the PTA meeting and say hello to someone. You have to get out of your comfort zone and take a trip to Samaria every once in a while.

Then, you also have to stay focused. One of my favorite parts of this story is often overlooked. In verse eight it says, *His disciples had gone into the town to buy food* ... (John 4:8 NIV). Verse six gives us the detail that it was about *the sixth hour*, which means it was lunchtime. They were hungry and since they stopped for a rest, the disciples had hurried off to get some fast food somewhere. While they were deliberating about which value meal to get, Jesus

---

[17] Hybels, Bill, *Just Walk Across the Room*. (Grand Rapids: Zondervan, 2006).

struck up a conversation with a woman. The disciples were focused on one thing, and Jesus was focused on something else. This point gets almost comical when the disciples returned from getting their food.

> Just then his disciples came back. They were shocked to find him talking to a woman, but none of them had the nerve to ask, "What do you want with her?" or "Why are you talking to her?" John 4:27 NLT

Then, the confusion increases in verse 31:

> Meanwhile, the disciples were urging Jesus, "Rabbi, eat something." But Jesus replied, "I have a kind of food you know nothing about." "Did someone bring him food while we were gone?" the disciples asked each other. Then Jesus explained: "My nourishment comes from doing the will of God, who sent me, and from finishing his work. (NLT)

Did you notice the misunderstanding? They were trying to get Jesus to eat the lunch they had purchased, and Jesus cryptically said, *I have food that you don't know anything about.* So they started wondering, did someone else bring Him food? Did He get something to eat while we were gone? But, of course, Jesus wasn't talking about physical food. He was talking about the spiritual nourishment that comes into your soul when you are fulfilling God's purpose. They were concerned about feeding their appetites, and Jesus was concerned about fulfilling God's purpose. They were concerned about the menu; He was concerned about ministry. They wanted food; He wanted people.

But then you really can't be too hard on the disciples. Don't we do it all the time? We are so focused on what we need to do—on eating, getting the errand finished, keeping our schedule—that we fail to see the opportunities to initiate potential relationships that are all around us. How many

Samaritan women have you just passed by and never noticed because you were on your way to lunch?

People see the things they are looking for. Jesus went everyday looking for opportunities to build relationships so that He could bring people to dynamic life. It's hard to *bring* if you don't first *build.*

One time I pastored a mission church that was located in a large field on what became a very busy road. In fact, it was called Racetrack Road. People would just fly by, and our church was in a small building set a good way off of the road. I went to work there nearly every day, and I was startled one day when a man stopped in. I greeted him at the door, and he held a paper cup in his hands that contained what looked like a ball of mud and a small flower inside. With an excited voice, he explained to me that this was a rare orchid. He had been driving down the road heading to south Florida and as he passed by, he explained, he saw this small flower in our field and he wanted to know if it was OK if he dug it up and took it with him. I told him it was fine with me. In fact, it looked like a weed to me, and I was hoping he would pick a few more of them.

As I went back inside somewhat amused by the whole thing, it occurred to me that this man was driving down a road headed somewhere hours south, driving probably 40-50 miles an hour or faster, and somehow he saw a rare orchid, no bigger than a hand, located in the middle of a 5-acre field. I went to work there every day, often walked around outside, and never once saw it and probably never would have. (And even if I had I wouldn't have appreciated it.) The difference between him and me was simple. He was looking for orchids; I wasn't. He was some kind of botanist. Everywhere he went he looked for orchids, and he knew one when he saw it. I never looked for them and wouldn't notice it if I saw it.

Do you know what the difference between Jesus and His disciples was that day? They both went to the same village, at the same time, and saw the same woman. The difference was that Jesus was looking for people. He saw an opportunity when it came along. The disciples were looking for food because that was their priority.

Of course, we have to eat, and there is nothing wrong with grabbing lunch out. But there is something wrong with going through life and not noticing the people all around us who need God. Your neighbors need God, your colleagues need God, your social friends need God, and the people you transact business with need God. Sometimes all you have to do is take the first step and build a relationship. Get to know their name, their family, and what is going on in their life. It doesn't have to start big, it can start small. It can be a step as small as saying, "Hello."

Why don't you begin to look for some people you can impact? Who needs to know about God? There are people in your sphere of influence that you can impact. There are people you can touch that maybe no one else can, at least no one quite like you. Look first at your immediate family. You already have a relationship with them. Does anyone in your immediate family need a relationship with God? Then look at your close friends and associates. Are there friends or colleagues whose relationship with God is uncertain? Do you know where they stand? Then there are people who you only know casually. Maybe you barely know a neighbor, or you see someone at a place of business on a regular basis. They are people in your life. They matter to God. If you don't know them well, then take the first step. Learn their name. Find out about their family. Your ability to contagiously influence others is tied to your willingness to take a step toward friendship. Make a list of people you want to influence and take the first step of friendship.

STEP TWO: DEMONSTRATE COMPASSION

People don't care how much you know until they know how much you care. Once you've started a relationship with someone, you need to look for ways to demonstrate that you really do care about them. Jesus did this by simply being willing to converse with a Samaritan woman in broad daylight. That simple act violated all the customs of the day; customs that had little to do with modesty but had everything to do with arrogance and self-righteousness, which are two things Jesus had no tolerance for. So He spoke to her, and she was surprised (John 4:9)

Sometimes just a conversation is all it takes to demonstrate compassion. Sometimes it takes more. Jesus said,

> *In the same way, let your light shine before men, that they may see your good deeds and praise your Father in heaven.*
> Matthew 5:16 NIV

Notice that it isn't our words that Jesus spoke of in this verse, but our deeds. Jesus said that our actions can demonstrate God's love to a watching world. Once you've started building a relationship with someone, ask yourself, "How can I demonstrate to that person that God is real, that He loves them, and so do I?"

I once heard of a pastor who moved in next to a spiritual skeptic. When his new neighbor heard that he was a pastor, the wall immediately went up and stayed up. Every attempt to turn a conversation toward spiritual things was immediately rebuffed. But over time the pastor looked for ways to demonstrate God's love. If he couldn't preach with words, he figured, he would do it with deeds. The thaw came when late one autumn he was cleaning the fallen leaves out of his gutters, and he realized that his neighbor's gutters were in pretty bad shape. His neighbor was elderly and unable to do it himself. One thing led to another and the pastor cleaned the gutters. The attitude began to thaw, the walls came down, and over time they were able to dialogue about spiritual things.

Unfortunately, many people have a negative view of church, faith, and all things that seem "religious." Maybe they have seen too many who said one thing and did another. Public scandals, fallen leaders, and hypocritical Christians all reinforce the worst stereotypes that some people have. And if that weren't enough, all you have to do is turn on some television stations to see preachers begging for money, manipulating people, and again reinforcing the very worst stereotypes. It is enough to embarrass those who are Christians and who really want to live for Christ.

The only way to overcome that is to demonstrate your compassion. It's hard not to like someone who really likes you. When you show someone that you care for them, respect them, like them for who they are, and care for them just as they are, over time the freeze can thaw and opportunities can arise. Just find a need and meet it.

Do you know what need everyone has? Everyone needs friends. We live in a culture where people are disconnected. Often people live hours or states away from their closest friends or family if they have them at all. Everyone needs friends.

Starting a friendship may be the greatest way to demonstrate your compassion to someone else. When is the last time you invited your neighbors over for a cookout? This could be called the barbecue principle. In their book *Becoming a Contagious Christian,* Bill Hybels and Mark Mittelberg talk about bringing the barbecue before you bring the Bible. Build the relationship before you try to bring them to church.[17] Sometimes that happens quickly, as in the story in John 4. Sometimes it happens slowly over weeks and months.

You may already have a relationship with someone, but it doesn't seem to be having much influence. Ask God to show you how to demonstrate compassion. Serve them at a point of need. Surprise them with an act of kindness. Open the door to a deeper friendship. Take the step. Take the risk. Jesus did. He demonstrated His love for us while we were still a long way from God (Romans 5:8).

What step will you take?

STEP THREE: COMMUNICATE THE GOSPEL

Truth must be shared. Directions must be given. A message must be heard. If not, what good is it? The gospel is a message about God. It is the truth about His love for us, our condition without Him, and what we must do to respond to Him. There are many ways to share spiritual truth. You can learn outlines and formulas, and they can be very helpful. After all, the more prepared we are, the more confident we will feel and the more likely we will be to share what we know.

Ultimately, it isn't an outline or a formula that needs to be shared; it is what you know about God's goodness. You are called to be a witness. Do you know what a witness is? A witness isn't an expert on every conceivable thing. He doesn't pretend to be an authority on every topic. A witness just tells what he knows. Tell what you know. Do the best you can and trust God to help you along the way. Jesus said, *For the Holy Spirit will teach you in that very hour what you ought to say* (Luke 12:12 NKJV).

---

[18]Hybels, Bill and Mark Mittelberg, *Becoming a Contagious Christian*. (Grand Rapids: Zondervan, 1994), 98.

Jesus spoke spiritual truth to the Samaritan woman in verse 14 when He said,

...whoever drinks the water I give him will never thirst. Indeed, the water I give him will become in him a spring of water welling up to eternal life. John 4:14 NIV

He continued a spiritual conversation with her that climaxed when she spoke of what she knew about the coming Messiah, and Jesus then revealed ultimate spiritual truth to her: He was the Messiah.

The woman said, "I know that Messiah" (called Christ) "is coming. When he comes, he will explain everything to us." Then Jesus declared, "I who speak to you am he." John 4:25-26 NIV

So, how do you communicate spiritual truth? Suppose the task falls to you to communicate the ultimate spiritual reality of life to an unbeliever. Can you do it? The answer is you can. Here are a couple of simple ways to think about communicating spiritual truth.

One way to think about it is that you are called to tell your story. Tell how God changed your life. The training curriculum *Becoming a Contagious Christian* suggests using an outline much like an outline of history. History is divided into two parts, BC and AD, to talk about the years *Before Christ* and *Anno Domini* (Latin for "In the year of (Our) Lord") for the years after Christ.[18] They are separated, of course, by the life of Jesus Himself. It's kind of neat, isn't it? Jesus divided history in two!

---

[19] Mittelberg, Mark, Lee Strobel, and Bill Hybels, *Becoming a Contagious Christian: Six Sessions on Communicating Your Faith in a Style that Fits You.* (Grand Rapids: Zondervan, 2007).

Tell about your life before Christ. Look for a theme that describes what your life was like before you knew Christ. Don't glamorize the past, and don't go into too much gory detail, but remember what it was like before you knew you were forgiven. Were you afraid, confused, guilt ridden, addicted, angry, or bitter? What was it you sensed that you needed?

Then, tell about how you met Christ. What was it the Holy Spirit used to show you your need for forgiveness? How did you hear about Jesus? How did you respond? Avoid churchy phrases that won't connect to people outside of church. Use clear simple words that can help outsiders know how to respond to the grace of God.

Then, tell about the difference Jesus made. Again, keep it brief, but point out that Jesus transformed your life. He gave you forgiveness, assurance, peace, and purpose. It's your story; tell it. Don't pretend to be perfect—you're not. Don't act like you don't have any problems—you do. But talk about the strength and direction that Jesus has given you. BC, Jesus, and then AD (which for us can mean "after my decision"). Tell your story. Make it brief, interesting, sincere and real. That is what the Samaritan woman did. She still wasn't even sure of Jesus' identity when she went back into town and simply told what she knew. And God used her story in a remarkable way. The Bible says people came from the town because of her invitation.

Then, leaving her water jar, the woman went back to the town and said to the people, "Come, see a man who told me everything I ever did. Could this be the Christ?" They came out of the town and made their way toward him. John 4:28-30 NIV

Jesus stayed two more days and at the end of the time, the Bible says, many people believed in Him. At the end of the story many people said to the woman,

We no longer believe just because of what you said; now we have heard for ourselves, and we know that this man really is the Savior of the world. John 4:42 NIV

Now, chances are you know even more than that woman did. You've probably heard sermons, sat through lessons, and perhaps even read the Bible. You know enough to change someone's life. You just have to be willing to tell your story.

The second way to think of communicating spiritual truth is to share His story. Just share the basic facts of the gospel. What is the gospel? What is the essence of the message that must be shared? I like to think that the essential gospel is the truth about four things.

It is the truth *about God*. The Bible teaches us that God is the one true God. He is the Creator of all, holy and perfect in all His ways. He is also a God who loves us and cares for us.

It is the truth about *mankind.* We are made in God's image. We are spiritual being made to know and serve God. However, all persons have sinned and fallen short of God's standard. Our sins have separated us from God and brought many bad things into our lives and into our world.

It is the truth about *Jesus.* Jesus is divine. He is God's Son, which means He is the very essence of God in a human form. God became man in order to rescue us. Jesus lived a perfect life and then died as a substitute for our sin on the cross. He rose from the dead, ascended into heaven, and He will one day return to reign forever. Jesus is Lord.

It is the truth about *salvation.* The gospel tells me that I can be saved through Jesus. I must trust Him. I put my faith in Him and ask Him to forgive me and take control of my life. If a person puts their faith in Christ and turns from their sin to follow Him, they are made right with God and begin a relationship with Him that will last forever.

This is what the gospel is: sharing the truth about God, man, Jesus, and salvation. What is the best way to share the gospel? The truth is there are many ways. Jesus used many different approaches depending on the person and the circumstance. When He spoke to the Samaritan woman He spoke of drinking living water; when He spoke to Nicodemus in John 3 He spoke of being born again; when He spoke to a rich young leader in Luke 18 He spoke of leaving everything behind to follow Christ. It is important to know the essence of the gospel so that you can share it in different ways at different times.

However, it is helpful to learn some basic ways to present the spiritual truth of the gospel. A simple way I like to use is the acrostic L.I.F.E.

L.I.F.E.

Jesus said, "I have come that they may have life ..." (John 10:10a NIV). In your conversation, share that the Bible says that Jesus has come to offer us real life. Then use the acrostic L.I.F.E. to explain what that means.

Love

God loves you and wants you to enjoy a personal relationship with Him. *For God so loved the world that he gave his one and only Son ...* (John 3:16a NIV).

Isolation

We are separated from God because of our sin. *For all have sinned and fall short of the glory of God* (Romans 3:23 NKJV) and *But there is a problem — your sins have cut you off from God* (Isaiah 59:2 NLT).

Forgiveness

Jesus died on the cross and rose again to pay the penalty of sin so you can experience complete forgiveness and eternal life. *In whom we have redemption through His blood, the forgiveness of sins* (Colossians 1:14 NKJV).

Eternal Life

When we place our trust in Jesus, we receive the gift of eternal life. *These things I have written to you who believe in the name of the Son of God, that you may know that you have eternal life* (1 John 5:13 NKJV).

ROMAN'S ROAD

Another way is to share some key verses from the book of Romans. This is sometimes called the Roman's Road. Mark your Bible, or memorize these easy verses which are found in Romans, and use them to explain the simple facts of the gospel.

Explain that everybody has failed (sinned) in some way and needs to be forgiven by God. *For all have sinned and fall short of the glory of God...* (Romans 3:23 NIV).

Explain that God loves us even though we are not perfect, and that He sent Jesus into the world to pay the price for our sins. *But God demonstrates His own love toward us, in that while we were still sinners, Christ died for us* (Romans 5:8 NIV).

Explain that while the consequences of sin are serious and eternal, God has offered us the gift of eternal life through Jesus. *For the wages of sin is death, but the gift of God is eternal life in Christ Jesus our Lord* (Romans 6:23 NIV).

Explain that we can receive God's forgiveness and salvation by confessing Jesus as our Lord and putting our trust in Him to save and forgive us.

*That if you confess with your mouth the Lord Jesus and believe
in your heart that God has raised Him from the dead, you will
be saved. For with the heart one believes unto righteousness,
and with the mouth confession is made unto salvation.*
Romans 10:9-10 NIV

For whoever calls on the name of the LORD shall be saved.
Romans 10:13 NKJV

Once you've shared your story or His story with
someone, you might finish the conversation by asking,
"Does this make sense to you?" If they seem open and even
willing to respond to Christ, you can lead them toward a
decision by asking, "Would you be willing to trust Christ
and receive His forgiveness right now?" If they are, lead
them in a prayer or offer to pray with them. Remember, this
isn't a magic prayer that manipulates God. God looks at our
hearts and helps us with the right words to say. A simple
prayer for forgiveness might sound like this.

*Dear God, thank you for making me and loving me. I admit
that I have sinned and that I need your forgiveness. I believe
you came for me in Jesus and died on the cross, rose again, and
that you are the Lord of all. Please forgive me and take control
of my life. I want to follow you from now on.*

God has blessed you to bless others. He has saved
you to use you. There are more who need to know about
Jesus and His love. In fact, the whole world needs to know
about Jesus. The only question is, "Will you let God use
you?"

Jesus finished the encounter with the Samaritan
woman by challenging His disciples. It was a lesson they
would never forget, and they would spend the rest of their
lives living it out.

*"My food," said Jesus, "is to do the will of him who sent me
and to finish his work. Do you not say, 'Four months more
and then the harvest'? I tell you, open your eyes and look at
the fields! They are ripe for harvest. Even now the reaper
draws his wages, even now he harvests the crop for eternal
life."* John 4:34-36 NIV

In Isaiah 6, the prophet Isaiah heard God's call. He
responded,

*Then I heard the voice of the Lord saying, "Whom shall I send?
And who will go for us?" And I said, "Here am I. Send me!"*
Isaiah 6:8 NIV

You can spend your life any way you want, but you
can only spend it once. When you surrender your life to be
used by God to influence others, you are giving yourself to
the most important task on earth. There is nothing like
watching God work through you to touch other people. It is
life in all its fullness. It is dynamic life.

Growth Steps
Take these growth steps to discover dynamic life:
- Make an "impact list" of three to five people that you
  want to influence for Christ.
- Ask God to put one person on your heart that you
  need to initiate a relationship with.
- Demonstrate compassion with an act of service to
  someone you know. Ask God to make His love
  known through you.
- Learn to share your story. Practice telling your story
  using the outline BC—your life before Christ,
  Christ—how you met Christ, and AD—the difference
  Jesus has made in your life.

- Learn to share an outline of the gospel using the L-I-F-E acrostic.
- Memorize the verses of the Roman's Road.

Devotional Guide

Read through these passages over the next week and write your observations, questions, and applications to your life.

Monday:	2 Corinthians 5:14-21
Tuesday:	Luke 19:1-10
Wednesday:	Acts 20:17-27
Thursday:	Jonah 4:1-11
Friday:	Romans 10:9-17
Weekend:	Psalm 71; Acts 1:1-8

This Week's Memory Verse

Be wise in the way you act toward outsiders; make the most of every opportunity. Let your conversation be always full of grace, seasoned with salt, so that you may know how to answer everyone. Colossians 4:5-6 NIV

CONCLUSION

The Christian life is not a destination, but a process. As Richard Foster once put it, *We have come to the end of this study, but only to the beginning of our journey.* You have learned what dynamic life is all about. Yes, it is about trusting in Jesus, but it is also about growing in your faith. You have been challenged to spend time with God in Bible study and prayer. You have been shown the importance of Christian com-munity and the great benefit it brings you and God's church. You have been challenged to serve others passionately as the Good Samaritan showed you in Luke 10. You have learned to love through worship of the One True God. You have been inspired to invest in eternal things – things that last – as opposed to those things which will soon pass away. Finally, you have seen how God has chosen to partner with you to take the Gospel message to the ends of the earth.

These disciplines are not to be learned and then checked off as if they are something to complete never to be looked at again. They are lifelong disciplines that must be practiced for the rest of your life as you grow and continue to grow in Christ. These disciplines chart a path for you to walk for life's journey if you desire to become more like Jesus.

The question that remains is what will become of you now? You have been given the information, but will there be life transformation? It is now time for you to step out in faith to act on all God has revealed to you. With the promise of the Holy Spirit to guide you, you can accomplish all that God has in store. It is time to experience dynamic life in Christ.

---

[20] Foster, Richard, *Celebration of Discipline*. (Harper One, 1998).

RESOURCES

𝕼𝖚𝖎𝖙 𝕮𝖑𝖆𝖎𝖒 𝕯𝖊𝖊𝖉

This Quit Claim Deed, set forth this_____ day of _____,
20_____ in the county of _____ in the
state of _____.

From: _____
To: <u>The Lord Jesus Christ</u>

I (we) hereby transfer to the Lord the ownership of the following
cash, property, and other assets:

_____
_____
_____
_____
_____
_____
_____
_____
_____
_____
_____
_____
_____

Steward(s) of the above list: Witnesses:
Name: _____   _____
Signature:_____   _____

Name:_____   _____
Signature:_____   _____

This is not a binding legal document.